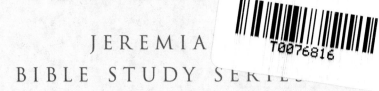

JEREMIAH
BIBLE STUDY SERIES

PHILIPPIANS

THE JOY OF LIVING IN CHRIST

DR. DAVID JEREMIAH

Prepared by Peachtree Publishing Services

HarperChristian
Resources

Philippians
Jeremiah Bible Study Series
© 2020 by Dr. David Jeremiah

Requests for information should be addressed to:
HarperChristian Resources, 3900 Sparks Dr. SE, Grand Rapids, Michigan 49546

ISBN 978-0-310-09170-7 (softcover)
ISBN 978-0-310-09171-4 (ebook)

HarperChristian Resources titles may be purchased in bulk for church, business, fundraising, or ministry use. For information, please e-mail ResourceSpecialist@ChurchSource.com.

Produced with assistance of Peachtree Publishing Service (www.PeachtreePublishingServices. com). Project staff include Christopher D. Hudson, Randy Southern, and Peter Blankenship.

First Printing May 2020 / Printed in the United States of America

23 24 25 26 27 LBC 10 9 8 7 6

CONTENTS

INTRODUCTION TO

The Letter to the Philippians

"I thank my God upon every remembrance of you, always in every prayer of mine making request for you all with joy . . . I have you in my heart, inasmuch as both in my chains and in the defense and confirmation of the gospel, you all are partakers with me of grace" (Philippians 1:3–4, 7). At the heart of Paul's letter to the Philippians is a message of thanksgiving and joy. He had found a group in the city of Philippi who had touched his heart. He had ministered to them and nurtured them in spiritual matters. In return, they had extended care and generosity to him—for which he was grateful. Yet Paul is also quick to note that he is writing this letter "in chains." He was in prison at the time, and he knew the believers would be facing hard times for their faith. So, he drafted this loving letter to prepare them for what lay ahead and to encourage them to persevere.

AUTHOR AND DATE

The writer of the letter identifies himself as the apostle Paul (see 1:1), and early church historians were nearly unanimous in identifying him as the author. The events depicted align with accounts given in Acts, and the theology aligns with Paul's teachings in his other letters. Luke tells us that Paul established the church in Philippi after being directed by the Holy Spirit to travel to Macedonia rather than go to Asia Minor (see Acts 16:6–10). It was there a woman named Lydia, "a seller of purple [cloth]" from the nearby city of Thyatira (verse 14), became one of his first converts—and thus one of the first converts in all of Europe. Paul composed the letter during one of his imprisonments, either AD 50 from Corinth, AD 53–55 from Ephesus, AD 58–59 from Caesarea—or, as most scholars believe, AD 60–62 from the city of Rome.

BACKGROUND AND SETTING

The city of Philippi was located along the Via Egnatia, a critical road that linked Rome with its eastern provinces, and was a center of trade. Paul established the church during his second missionary journey, and the church had become instrumental in supporting his ministry efforts. It appears that when the congregation heard Paul was in prison, they became concerned and sent a man named Epaphroditus to bring money to Paul and help in his time of need. Paul thus wrote this letter to thank the Philippians for their gift and to explain the significance of his imprisonment so the believers would not lose heart. Above all, Paul wanted them to learn to rejoice regardless of the circumstances they faced. In addition, the apostle had evidently heard of tensions brewing among certain members in the church so he wanted to remind all of the believers to remain unified as a community and bear with one another in love.

KEY THEMES

Several key themes are prominent in the letter to the Philippians. The first is that *believers are to be joyful* (see 1:3–30; 4:4–20). Paul introduces the believers to a contentment that is more profound than happiness. While happiness is a temporary state that comes and goes with moods and circumstances, joy runs deeper because its source is a personal relationship with Christ. As the believers drew their joy from the Lord, they would be able to find joy in any circumstance, for they were tapping into a source greater than their own.

A second theme is that *believers are to be united* (see 2:1–4). Paul uses words such as *fellowship* and *partakers* to stress his connection with the Philippians in their shared ministry. He expresses his gratitude for the Philippians' involvement in his ministry but also helps them realize their generosity is a benefit to them as well. He calls the believers to join with him in pressing on toward the goal and keeping their focus on heaven (see 3:12–21). He explains their gifts of service as a "sweet-smelling aroma, an acceptable sacrifice, well-pleasing to God" (4:18).

A third theme is that *believers are to be humble* (see 2:5–30). The apostle Paul helps the believers understand that God can accomplish extraordinary things through those who have a humble spirit. He offers the life of Christ as the ultimate example to follow, who "humbled Himself and became obedient to the point of death" (2:8). The believers are likewise to model humility in their relationships with one another and to do so "without complaining or disputing" (2:14).

A fourth theme is that *believers are to have wisdom*. Paul is concerned that the greatest strength of the Philippian believers—their love—could be exploited by unscrupulous teachers who had infiltrated the church. Some of these teachers were trying to convince the believers they needed to become Jews, through circumcision and strict obedience to the Law, before they could become Christians (see 3:2–6). Paul had battled such teachings in other churches, but he was concerned the Philippians were especially vulnerable because of their welcoming spirit. He urges them to exercise discernment in their dealings with others.

KEY APPLICATIONS

Philippians is a powerful reminder for us to keep our focus on Christ and follow His example as we deal with circumstances here on earth. As believers, we have received the gift of God's salvation, and everything else pales in comparison to that blessing. We therefore should never allow our moods or situation to steal our joy or take our focus off the work God has for us. Instead, we must seek to find joy in each and every situation that we face.

THE JOY OF COMMUNITY

Philippians 1:1–11

GETTING STARTED

Who are the people you are most thankful for in your life? Why are you thankful for them?

SETTING THE STAGE

As we read the opening words of Paul's letter to the Philippians, we are immediately struck by the joy and thankfulness the apostle felt for this community of believers. In the space of a few short verses, he shares that he is thankful to God whenever he thinks of them, how their example fills him with joy, how he values their fellowship, and how he longs to see them again.

For more than a decade, the members of this small church in the Roman colony of Philippi had flourished as a close-knit group of believers. The apostle Paul, who had founded the church some ten years before, simply could not hide the deep attachment he felt to them. Even though he had been separated from them due to his imprisonment, he wanted them to know they were still continually in his thoughts and prayers.

It can be a bit startling to think that this great man of God, who had accomplished so much in establishing the churches, was desperate for the fellowship of his Christian friends. But in truth, Paul was built just like us—and none of us were designed to do life on our own. God created us for fellowship and for relationship. He wanted their fellowship to continue in spite of the miles of separation that lay between them. He desired their love for one another to grow.

As Paul communicates his feelings for these believers, he touches on many of the prerequisites for loving relationships in any church. His words remind us that we should all be thankful for our fellow brothers and sisters. The question is . . . are we thankful for them?

EXPLORING THE TEXT

Greeting (Philippians 1:1–7)

---

¹ Paul and Timothy, bondservants of Jesus Christ,

    To all the saints in Christ Jesus who are in Philippi, with the bishops and deacons:

² Grace to you and peace from God our Father and the Lord Jesus Christ.

³ I thank my God upon every remembrance of you, ⁴ always in every prayer of mine making request for you all with joy, ⁵ for your fellowship in the gospel from the first day until now, ⁶ being confident of this very thing, that He who has begun a good work in you will complete it until the day of Jesus Christ; ⁷ just as it is right for me to think this of you all, because I have you in my heart, inasmuch as both in my chains and in the defense and confirmation of the gospel, you all are partakers with me of grace.

---

1. The opening line of first-century letters almost always included the name of the sender, the name of the recipient, and a general greeting. In this case, Paul indicates the letter is from him and Timothy (his co-worker), but adds that they are "bondservants of Christ" (verse 1). The Greek term for *bondservant* refers not to a hired servant but rather to a slave. What point is Paul making by identifying himself and Timothy in this manner?

2. Paul's greeting reveals a great deal about his relationship and past history with these believers. How would you describe his feelings toward them? How does he view them as partakers in his mission of spreading the gospel (see verses 3–7)?

_____

_____

_____

_____

_____

_____

_____

Thankfulness and Prayer (Philippians 1:8–11)

8 For God is my witness, how greatly I long for you all with the affection of Jesus Christ.

9 And this I pray, that your love may abound still more and more in knowledge and all discernment, 10 that you may approve the things that are excellent, that you may be sincere and without offense till the day of Christ, 11 being filled with the fruits of righteousness which are by Jesus Christ, to the glory and praise of God.

3. Paul next describes the content of his prayers for the Philippians. What does he ask God to provide to them? What does he hope this will accomplish in them (see verses 9–10)?

_____

_____

_____

_____

_____

_____

4. Paul uses the phrase "fruits of righteousness" to describe the work he wants God to do in the lives of the believers (see verse 11). How would you describe these fruits?

_____

_____

_____

_____

_____

_____

_____

GOING DEEPER

The picture that Paul paints of the church in Philippi is a congregation that loves one another, is growing in the faith together, and is supporting the work of spreading the gospel. In many ways, this church reflects the harmony that was experienced in the very first church in Jerusalem. Luke tells us the following about that church in the book of Acts.

A Vital Church Grows (Acts 2:41–47)

[41] Then those who gladly received [Peter's] word were baptized; and that day about three thousand souls were added to them. [42] And they continued steadfastly in the apostles' doctrine and fellowship, in the breaking of bread, and in prayers. [43] Then fear came upon every soul, and many wonders and signs were done through the apostles. [44] Now all who believed were together, and had all things in common, [45] and sold their possessions and goods, and divided them among all, as anyone had need.

[46] So continuing daily with one accord in the temple, and breaking bread from house to house, they ate their food with gladness and

simplicity of heart, ⁴⁷ praising God and having favor with all the people. And the Lord added to the church daily those who were being saved.

---

5. These events occurred shortly after Peter delivered a sermon in which he proclaimed Jesus to be the promised Messiah. How did the people respond to his message? What happened as a result—in spite of their different backgrounds (see verses 41–45)?

_____

_____

_____

_____

_____

_____

6. What traits characterized this early body of believers (see verses 46–47)? What similar traits did the believers in Philippi possess?

_____

_____

_____

_____

_____

_____

Paul's thankfulness for the believers in Philippi reveals the church was doing well in loving one another and supporting the mission of spreading the gospel. This was not the case in every church that Paul had helped to found. In the following letter, he instructs a group of believers that was struggling with unity and how the body of Christ is supposed to function.

Unity and Diversity in One Body (1 Corinthians 12:20–26)

20 But now indeed there are many members, yet one body. 21 And the eye cannot say to the hand, "I have no need of you"; nor again the head to the feet, "I have no need of you." 22 No, much rather, those members of the body which seem to be weaker are necessary. 23 And those members of the body which we think to be less honorable, on these we bestow greater honor; and our unpresentable parts have greater modesty, 24 but our presentable parts have no need. But God composed the body, having given greater honor to that part which lacks it, 25 that there should be no schism in the body, but that the members should have the same care for one another. 26 And if one member suffers, all the members suffer with it; or if one member is honored, all the members rejoice with it.

7. Some of the believers in Corinth thought they possessed spiritual gifts that were more important than the other gifts—which was leading to issues of pride. How does Paul emphasize the importance of *every* member of the body of Christ (see verses 20–24)?

8. Why is it important for believers to support and encourage one another (see verses 25–26)?

_____

_____

_____

_____

_____

_____

_____

REVIEWING THE STORY

Paul opens his letter by expressing his love and affection for the believers in Philippi—a community that had continually supported his work in sharing the gospel. He states that he is thankful for their fellowship and is confident that God will continue to mature them in the faith. Although he is in prison, their partnership with him in sharing the gospel brings him comfort. He prays that their love for one another will continue to abound, that they will gain knowledge and discernment to identify false teaching, and that they will continue to lead godly lives.

9. How does Paul refer to himself and Timothy (see Philippians 1:1)?

_____

_____

_____

_____

_____

_____

10. What was the "very thing" that Paul was confident of concerning his brothers and sisters in Christ in Philippi (see Philippians 1:6)?

_____

_____

_____

_____

_____

_____

11. What did Paul pray would guide the believers' abounding love (see Philippians 1:9)?

_____

_____

_____

_____

_____

_____

12. What did Paul want the Philippian believers to approve (see Philippians 1:10)?

_____

_____

_____

_____

_____

APPLYING THE MESSAGE

13. How are you expressing your love to the Christians who have made—and are making—a difference in your life?

_____

_____

_____

_____

_____

_____

_____

_____

_____

_____

14. What are some ways that you can become more involved in your community of believers?

_____

_____

_____

_____

_____

_____

_____

_____

_____

_____

REFLECTING ON THE MEANING

Scholars tell us that Philippians is the most personal and intimate letter in the Bible. Although the letter consists of just four chapters, there are more than 100 occurrences of the words *I, me,* and *my.* In fact, the word *I* alone occurs fifty-two times! As Paul addresses the people of Philippi in the first few verses, we can feel the depth of his affection: "I thank my God upon every remembrance of you . . . I have you in my heart . . . I long for you all" (1:3, 7–8).

Paul could have just kept these feelings to himself. After all, he and the believers in Philippi had been partnering together for years. Shouldn't they know by now how he felt? Yet Paul knew that unexpressed love is useless when it comes to ministering to a community. The believers in Philippi *needed* to hear these words from Paul. They needed to know that he recognized their sacrifice and appreciated all they had given to him.

A commercial that ran several years ago pictured a scene between a father and son. The son said, "I love you," but the dad couldn't physically hear the words. In the next scene, the father now has a hearing aid. The son again tells his dad, "I love you," . . . but again the man doesn't respond. So the son repeats the words: "Dad, I love you." The father replies, "I heard you the first time, son, but I just wanted to hear it twice."

Don't we all feel that way? No one is guaranteed tomorrow, so we need to express our love and appreciation for others *today.* We need to follow the example that Paul sent in each of his letters: "I thank my God always concerning you" (1 Corinthians 1:4); "I . . . do not cease to give thanks for you" (Ephesians 1:15–16), "We give thanks to God, the Father of our Lord Jesus Christ, praying always for you" (Colossians 1:3); "We give thanks to God always for you all, making mention of you in our prayers" (1 Thessalonians 1:2).

Somebody once said that if you are full of gratitude, you can't be angry at anybody. Likewise, if your heart is filled with thanksgiving, it won't be hard for you to express your feelings of love and affection for the people in your life.

11

JOURNALING YOUR RESPONSE

How can you nurture a spirit of gratitude in your life?

THE JOY OF ADVERSITY

Philippians 1:12–18

GETTING STARTED

How have you been able to help others because of the challenges that you have faced?

_____

_____

_____

_____

_____

_____

_____

_____

_____

_____

_____

_____

SETTING THE STAGE

The apostle Paul was no stranger to adversity . . . or to prisons. In the book of Acts, we read that he was arrested in Philippi (see 16:16–40) and in Jerusalem (see 21:27–36). We also know from Paul's own writings that he was arrested at least a third time, as in four of his epistles—Ephesians, Philippians, Colossians, and Philemon—he speaks of being in chains. As he said to the Corinthians, "Are they ministers of Christ? . . . I am more: in labors more abundant, in stripes above measure, in prisons more frequently" (2 Corinthians 11:23).

Scholars believe that Paul experienced a wide variety of conditions in these Roman prisons. He was chained in a common holding cell in Philippi. He likely received better conditions while being held after his arrest in Jerusalem. In Rome, he evidently lived in relative comfort while under house arrest and could receive visitors (see Acts 28:16–17). But by the time he wrote Philippians, the apostle was considered an enemy of the state. It is likely that he was placed in an underground prison in Rome. He was possibly held at the Roman Mamertine Prison, where enemies of the government were held before they were executed.

Paul could have become bitter and hardened against God as a result of these imprisonments. But as he reveals in Philippians, he saw his adversity as a means for "the furtherance of the gospel" (1:12), for as a result of his arrest, the whole palace guard had been exposed to the message of Christ! For Paul, to live was to share the gospel and bring people into God's kingdom, but to die was to step into God's kingdom and receive his reward.

Paul's example reveals that God often will often allow adversity to come into the lives of His servants. While we cannot control these circumstances, we can control how we react to them. We can, like Paul, choose to believe that God is working even in the midst of our trials.

EXPLORING THE TEXT

Chains in Christ (Philippians 1:12–14)

---

12 But I want you to know, brethren, that the things which happened to me have actually turned out for the furtherance of the gospel, 13 so that it has become evident to the whole palace guard, and to all the rest, that my chains are in Christ; 14 and most of the brethren

in the Lord, having become confident by my chains, are much more bold to speak the word without fear.

---

1. Paul was often falsely accused of inciting people to oppose Roman law (see Acts 16:20; 17:7; 18:12–17). It is likely these same charges had been brought against him and led to this arrest. But what does Paul say the Roman guards had come to realize about the *real* reason for his imprisonment (see verse 13)?

_____

_____

_____

_____

2. It is likely the Romans authorities believed that by arresting Paul, they would frighten his fellow Christians into silence. Instead, what impact did Paul's "chains" have on most of them (see verse 14)?

_____

_____

_____

_____

Christ Is Preached (Philippians 1:15–18)

[15] Some indeed preach Christ even from envy and strife, and some also from goodwill: [16] The former preach Christ from selfish ambition, not sincerely, supposing to add affliction to my chains; [17] but the latter out of love, knowing that I am appointed for the defense of the gospel. [18] What then? Only that in every way, whether in pretense or in truth, Christ is preached; and in this I rejoice, yes, and will rejoice.

---

3. Paul sees his imprisonment as serving to embolden his fellow teachers and advance the gospel. However, he is aware that not all of these teachers share his same motives. What two groups of teachers does he identify (see verses 15–17)?

_____

_____

_____

_____

4. Many of Paul's rivals were benefiting from his imprisonment now that he was off the scene. What surprising response does Paul have to their work (see verse 18)?

_____

_____

_____

_____

GOING DEEPER

Paul had a special ability to view his adversity and suffering as serving a greater purpose—to advance the gospel throughout the world. In the book of Genesis, we read how Joseph also endured trials and setbacks, yet in the end could also see how God had used his struggle for the greater good. At the end of his journey, he could look back and relate the following to his brothers, who years before had sold him into slavery in Egypt.

Joseph Reassures His Brothers (Genesis 50:15–21)

15 When Joseph's brothers saw that their father was dead, they said, "Perhaps Joseph will hate us, and may actually repay us for all the evil which we did to him." 16 So they sent messengers to Joseph,

saying, "Before your father died he commanded, saying, [17] 'Thus you shall say to Joseph: "I beg you, please forgive the trespass of your brothers and their sin; for they did evil to you." ' Now, please, forgive the trespass of the servants of the God of your father." And Joseph wept when they spoke to him.

[18] Then his brothers also went and fell down before his face, and they said, "Behold, we are your servants."

[19] Joseph said to them, "Do not be afraid, for am I in the place of God? [20] But as for you, you meant evil against me; but God meant it for good, in order to bring it about as it is this day, to save many people alive. [21] Now therefore, do not be afraid; I will provide for you and your little ones." And he comforted them and spoke kindly to them.

---

5. Joseph had endured a great deal of suffering at the hands of his brothers. What fears did they have when their father died? What plan did they put together (see verses 15–17)?

_____

_____

_____

_____

6. How did Joseph respond to his brothers' words (see verses 19–21)? How does his attitude toward adversity match up with what we see in the apostle Paul?

_____

_____

_____

_____

Paul recognized that suffering and persecution were a reality not only for him but also for all believers who seek to share the gospel of Christ. His message to the Philippians was to not allow this reality to discourage them but actually embolden them to share their faith. Other teachers in the early church shared this view, as the following passage illustrates.

Suffering for God's Glory (1 Peter 4:12–16)

[12] Beloved, do not think it strange concerning the fiery trial which is to try you, as though some strange thing happened to you; [13] but rejoice to the extent that you partake of Christ's sufferings, that when His glory is revealed, you may also be glad with exceeding joy. [14] If you are reproached for the name of Christ, blessed are you, for the Spirit of glory and of God rests upon you. On their part He is blasphemed, but on your part He is glorified. [15] But let none of you suffer as a murderer, a thief, an evildoer, or as a busybody in other people's matters. [16] Yet if anyone suffers as a Christian, let him not be ashamed, but let him glorify God in this matter.

7. What attitude does Peter urge believers to avoid when they experience trials? What attitude are they to adopt (see verses 12–13)?

_____

_____

_____

8. How are believers to respond when they are persecuted for their faith? Why can they consider themselves *blessed* if this happens (see verses 14–16)?

_____

_____

_____

_____

REVIEWING THE STORY

Paul urges the believers to find joy in their adversity. He states that his imprisonment has served to advance the gospel, for his palace guard has been exposed to the message of salvation. Others have become emboldened by his example to speak the word of Christ without fear. Paul acknowledges that not all teachers do this for the best reason. But regardless of their motives, he chooses to rejoice that the gospel is being shared.

9. What did Paul want the believers to know about his situation (see Philippians 1:12)?

_____

_____

_____

_____

_____

_____

_____

10. What had become evident to the whole palace guard (see Philippians 1:13)?

_____

_____

_____

_____

_____

_____

_____

11. What did Paul recognize about his divine appointment (see Philippians 1:17)?

_____

_____

_____

_____

_____

_____

12. In what could Paul ultimately rejoice (see Philippians 1:18)?

_____

_____

_____

_____

_____

_____

APPLYING THE MESSAGE

13. What adversity are you facing right now?

_____

_____

_____

_____

_____

_____

14. How might God bring good from your adversity?

_____

_____

_____

_____

_____

_____

REFLECTING ON THE MEANING

The apostle Paul makes an interesting observation when he writes, "Some indeed preach Christ even from envy and strife, and some also from goodwill: The former preach Christ from selfish ambition, not sincerely, supposing to add affliction to my chains" (1:15–16). As we have seen, Paul was in prison when he wrote this letter, but he was still able to receive information from his friends. They told him some of his associates were taking advantage of his imprisonment to advance their careers. They were using Paul's adversity to make things better for themselves.

Paul says these individuals were preaching from "selfish ambition." The phrase basically means they were "canvasing for office" to get people to support them. They were preaching the gospel with the aim of getting people to follow _them_ rather than getting people to follow _Christ_. These were godly teachers who were acting in ungodly ways. But notice how Paul responds to the news of these teachers. He does not rail against them or send somebody to correct them. Instead, he rejoices that Christ is being preached. He knows that while God might not honor the motive of the messenger, He will always honor the message being preached.

Times of adversity will reveal who our true friends are in this world. However, as we see in the case of the apostle Paul, such times will also reveal our true _priorities_ in this world. God will use adversity as a lens to sharpen our focus on Him and His mission for us. In the end, we will find that some of the things we thought were important are actually insignificant. We will be able to let those things go—just as Paul was able to do—so we can concentrate all of our efforts on fulfilling what we recognize to be God's greater plans for our days on this earth.

JOURNALING YOUR RESPONSE

How can you help someone who is facing adversity?

THE JOY OF INTEGRITY

Philippians 1:19–30

GETTING STARTED

What does it mean to have integrity?

_____

_____

_____

_____

_____

_____

_____

_____

_____

_____

_____

_____

_____

_____

_____

_____

_____

_____

_____

_____

SETTING THE STAGE

The apostle Paul understood the importance of integrity. He had faced accusations from rivals throughout his ministry and had been forced to defend his motives on more than one occasion. Fortunately, due to his integrity, he was always able to point to the example of his life as his best defense. As he wrote to one congregation, "You are witnesses, and God also, how devoutly and justly and blamelessly we behaved ourselves among you" (1 Thessalonians 2:10).

Integrity is just as critical for us. In fact, many executives today factor in a candidate's integrity when it comes to making a hiring decision. One executive at a major car manufacturing company asks three key questions to help her determine how candidates value integrity. First, she asks how their *peers* would describe them. Next, she asks how their *supervisors* would describe them. Finally, she asks how their *subordinates* would describe them. According to the executive, the best candidates are those whose answers do not change much from description to description. The best candidates are those who practice integrity at every level in their lives.

The word *integrity* actually comes from the word *integral*, which means "one." If we have integrity, we have a *sameness* to us. We don't change because of where we are or what we are facing. Even when challenges come our way—as they did for Paul—we respond in a manner that lets others know they can trust us and depend on us. This was the message Paul wanted to communicate in this next section. He knew the trials he was facing would soon come to the believers. He wanted to prepare them . . . and us . . . on how to respond with integrity.

EXPLORING THE TEXT

To Live Is Christ (Philippians 1:19–26)

19 For I know that this will turn out for my deliverance through your prayer and the supply of the Spirit of Jesus Christ, 20 according to my

earnest expectation and hope that in nothing I shall be ashamed, but with all boldness, as always, so now also Christ will be magnified in my body, whether by life or by death. [21] For to me, to live is Christ, and to die is gain. [22] But if I live on in the flesh, this will mean fruit from my labor; yet what I shall choose I cannot tell. [23] For I am hard-pressed between the two, having a desire to depart and be with Christ, which is far better. [24] Nevertheless to remain in the flesh is more needful for you. [25] And being confident of this, I know that I shall remain and continue with you all for your progress and joy of faith, [26] that your rejoicing for me may be more abundant in Jesus Christ by my coming to you again.

---

1. According to Paul, what two means would God use to secure his deliverance? What did Paul hope that he would be able to continue to do even while in prison (see verses 19–20)?

---

2. What conclusions does Paul reach as he compares his options of living or dying? Why does he say that he is "hard-pressed" between the two (see verses 21–24)?

Striving and Suffering for Christ (Philippians 1:27–30)

[27] Only let your conduct be worthy of the gospel of Christ, so that whether I come and see you or am absent, I may hear of your affairs,

that you stand fast in one spirit, with one mind striving together for the faith of the gospel, [28] and not in any way terrified by your adversaries, which is to them a proof of perdition, but to you of salvation, and that from God. [29] For to you it has been granted on behalf of Christ, not only to believe in Him, but also to suffer for His sake, [30] having the same conflict which you saw in me and now hear is in me.

---

3. The apostle Paul, having reassured the believers that he is standing strong in the midst of persecution, now wants to make sure they are doing the same thing. Why was it important for them to maintain a united and consistent front (see verses 27–28)?

_____

_____

_____

_____

_____

4. Believers in Christ are granted God's mercy, grace, and forgiveness at salvation. However, what does Paul say that believers are also "granted on behalf of Christ" (see verses 29–30)?

_____

_____

_____

_____

Going Deeper

The Bible is filled with examples of people like Paul who were able to maintain their integrity under pressure. In the Old Testament, we read how Daniel was carried into captivity and forced to endure the pressures of a foreign culture . . . and plots against him. However, as the following story relates, Daniel continued to honor God with his choices and his behavior.

Daniel's Training in Babylon (Daniel 1:8–14)

8 But Daniel purposed in his heart that he would not defile himself with the portion of the king's delicacies, nor with the wine which he drank; therefore he requested of the chief of the eunuchs that he might not defile himself. 9 Now God had brought Daniel into the favor and goodwill of the chief of the eunuchs. 10 And the chief of the eunuchs said to Daniel, "I fear my lord the king, who has appointed your food and drink. For why should he see your faces looking worse than the young men who are your age? Then you would endanger my head before the king."

11 So Daniel said to the steward whom the chief of the eunuchs had set over Daniel, Hananiah, Mishael, and Azariah, 12 "Please test your servants for ten days, and let them give us vegetables to eat and water to drink. 13 Then let our appearance be examined before you, and the appearance of the young men who eat the portion of the king's delicacies; and as you see fit, so deal with your servants." 14 So he consented with them in this matter, and tested them ten days.

5. How did Daniel demonstrate his integrity when he was chosen to serve Nebuchadnezzar, the king of Babylon (see verse 8)?

6. How did Daniel show his integrity in dealing with the chief of the eunuchs and the steward (see verses 10–14)?

_____

_____

_____

_____

Daniel and His Friends Obey God (Daniel 1:15–21)

15 And at the end of ten days their features appeared better and fatter in flesh than all the young men who ate the portion of the king's delicacies. 16 Thus the steward took away their portion of delicacies and the wine that they were to drink, and gave them vegetables.

17 As for these four young men, God gave them knowledge and skill in all literature and wisdom; and Daniel had understanding in all visions and dreams.

18 Now at the end of the days, when the king had said that they should be brought in, the chief of the eunuchs brought them in before Nebuchadnezzar. 19 Then the king interviewed them, and among them all none was found like Daniel, Hananiah, Mishael, and Azariah; therefore they served before the king. 20 And in all matters of wisdom and understanding about which the king examined them, he found them ten times better than all the magicians and astrologers who were in all his realm. 21 Thus Daniel continued until the first year of King Cyrus.

7. How did God reward the integrity of Daniel and his friends (see verses 15–17)?

_____

_____

_____

_____

8. How did their integrity put them into positions of influence (see verses 18–20)?

_____

_____

_____

_____

REVIEWING THE STORY

The apostle Paul reassures his readers that his imprisonment will result in deliverance—either on this side of earth or in eternity. He stresses that his goal, as always, is to glorify Christ regardless of whether he lives or dies. He is torn between the two options, for he desires to be with God in heaven, but also desires to keep bringing people to salvation. He concludes by encouraging the believers to maintain their integrity, so that they will be able to stand strong and not be discouraged when the trials and persecutions he is facing come their way.

9. What did Paul want to happen whether he lived or died (see Philippians 1:20)?

_____

_____

_____

_____

10. Which option did Paul see as "far better" when it came to living or dying (Philippians 1:23)?

_____

_____

_____

_____

11. What is the standard that believers should strive for in conduct (see Philippians 1:27)?

_____

_____

_____

_____

_____

_____

12. How did the adversaries of the believers view the gospel (see Philippians 1:28)?

_____

_____

_____

_____

_____

_____

APPLYING THE MESSAGE

13. What are some of the benefits that you have received from living with integrity?

_____

_____

_____

_____

_____

_____

14. What is a specific area in your life where you can demonstrate greater integrity?

_____

_____

_____

_____

_____

REFLECTING ON THE MEANING

In this section of Philippians, Paul instructs the believers to let their "conduct be worthy of the gospel of Christ" (1:27). The Greek word translated *conduct* is *politeuo* or *polis*, which is the word for *city*. In the Greek language, the word meant the citizens who belong to a city. *Conduct*, as it is portrayed in this verse, thus refers to the public duties of good citizens.

The Philippians would have understood this concept well. Philippi was a Roman colony, but it was located 800 miles away from Rome. The citizens of Philippi were thus citizens of Rome, but they were removed from that great city. Even so, they knew the emperor expected them to represent Rome in their culture in a way that would not embarrass the empire.

Paul is saying, in effect, "Just as you in Philippi are a colony of Rome, you are also citizens of another place. You are citizens of heaven." As he will later state, "Our citizenship is in heaven, from which we also eagerly wait for the Savior" (3:20). Just as the Philippians were to represent Rome well as a colony of the empire, so the believers were to represent Christ well as ambassadors for God's eternal kingdom. They were to conduct themselves in a way that was worthy of the calling they had received and bring glory to God.

Each day, our goal should be to live as citizens of heaven. If we were to do this, people would recognize that we possess different perspectives and priorities from the rest of the world. Our lives would cause us to stand out and point people to the truth that is found in Christ.

JOURNALING YOUR RESPONSE

What unique differences are people seeing in the way you conduct your life?

THE JOY OF UNITY

Philippians 2:1–11

GETTING STARTED

What is something you accomplished in your life only through working on a team?

_____

_____

_____

_____

_____

_____

_____

_____

_____

_____

_____

_____

_____

_____

_____

_____

_____

SETTING THE STAGE

In this next section of the letter, the apostle Paul transitions from speaking about his own situation to speaking about the situation taking place in the church in Philippi. He begins with a topic familiar in many of his letters: *unity in the body of Christ*. Paul states that if the believers are concerned for his welfare, they can fulfill his joy by being likeminded and unified.

Paul was being immensely practical in stressing this point. He knew that more could be accomplished for the work of the gospel if the believers were working together toward the same goal. It's a principle illustrated in an old parable of a man with three feuding sons. The father called them together, handed the oldest son a bundle of sticks, and said, "break them." The oldest son tried as hard as he could, but he could not break the bundle.

The old man then handed the bundle to his middle son. "Break them," he again instructed. Like his older brother, the young man could not break the bundle. When the father turned to his youngest son, the boy was ready for the challenge. He untied the bundle and broke each stick individually with little effort. "You have proven my point," the old man said. "You are like the bundle of sticks. Separately, you are vulnerable and can be broken. Together, you are strong."

There is power when believers come together and work together for a common cause. Also, as Paul well knew, there is strength. "Though one may be overpowered by another, two can withstand him . . . a threefold cord is not quickly broken" (Ecclesiastes 4:12).

EXPLORING THE TEXT

Unity Through Humility (Philippians 2:1–4)

---

¹ Therefore if there is any consolation in Christ, if any comfort of love, if any fellowship of the Spirit, if any affection and mercy, ² fulfill my joy by being like-minded, having the same love, being of one accord, of one mind. ³ Let nothing be done through selfish ambition or conceit,

but in lowliness of mind let each esteem others better than himself.
[4] Let each of you look out not only for his own interests, but also for
the interests of others.

---

1. Paul has just addressed issues related to outside persecutions that
threatened to tear apart the church. Now he will address the internal
conflicts . . . which can be just as dangerous. What does Paul say the
Philippians need to do to make his joy complete (see verses 1–2)?

_____

_____

_____

_____

_____

_____

2. The Roman culture of the day encouraged its citizens to strive
constantly for personal honor and glory. What attitude does Paul
recommend the Philippians embrace in order to prevent this attitude
of egotism from polluting their unity (see verses 3–4)?

_____

_____

_____

_____

_____

_____

_____

The Humbled and Exalted Christ (Philippians 2:5–11)

⁵ Let this mind be in you which was also in Christ Jesus, ⁶ who, being in the form of God, did not consider it robbery to be equal with God, ⁷ but made Himself of no reputation, taking the form of a bond-servant, and coming in the likeness of men. ⁸ And being found in appearance as a man, He humbled Himself and became obedient to the point of death, even the death of the cross. ⁹ Therefore God also has highly exalted Him and given Him the name which is above every name, ¹⁰ that at the name of Jesus every knee should bow, of those in heaven, and of those on earth, and of those under the earth, ¹¹ and that every tongue should confess that Jesus Christ is Lord, to the glory of God the Father.

---

3. Scholars believe that most of this passage is taken from an early Christian hymn that Paul adapted for his purposes. What does Paul state about Jesus as it relates to humility (see verses 5–8)?

4. Paul states that Jesus led a life of humility and was exalted by God. In the same way, God will honor those believers who live with humility. What does Paul remind the believers here about the coming day of judgment, when God will weigh the actions of those who continually sought only their own honor and glory (see verses 9–11)?

_____

_____

_____

_____

_____

_____

_____

_____

_____

_____

_____

GOING DEEPER

Paul's teaching on the power of unity is a principle that goes back to Old Testament times. Solomon, the wisest man to ever live, expounded on this same idea in the book of Ecclesiastes. His words remind us that two working together are truly better than one working alone.

Two Are Better Than One (Ecclesiastes 4:8–12)

> [8] There is one alone, without companion:
> He has neither son nor brother.
> Yet there is no end to all his labors,
> Nor is his eye satisfied with riches.

But he never asks,

"For whom do I toil and deprive myself of good?"

This also is vanity and a grave misfortune.

⁹ Two are better than one,

Because they have a good reward for their labor.

¹⁰ For if they fall, one will lift up his companion.

But woe to him who is alone when he falls,

For he has no one to help him up.

¹¹ Again, if two lie down together, they will keep warm;

But how can one be warm alone?

¹² Though one may be overpowered by another, two can withstand him.

And a threefold cord is not quickly broken.

---

5. How does Solomon describe those who focus only on their own goals (see verse 8)? How can these words be applied to unity among believers in the church?

6. What are some of the benefits of two working together? How does unity bring both security and strength (see verses 9–12)?

_____

_____

_____

_____

_____

_____

_____

Paul's call for unity among the Philippians can also be found in Jesus' call for His followers to seek unity. Jesus knew that unity would provide the strength His followers needed when persecution arose or false teachers tried to lead them astray. In the following prayer, He recognized the power Christian unity carries—not just among believers but also in the world.

Jesus Prays for All Believers (John 17:20–26)

20 "I do not pray for these alone, but also for those who will believe in Me through their word; 21 that they all may be one, as You, Father, are in Me, and I in You; that they also may be one in Us, that the world may believe that You sent Me. 22 And the glory which You gave Me I have given them, that they may be one just as We are one: 23 I in them, and You in Me; that they may be made perfect in one, and that the world may know that You have sent Me, and have loved them as You have loved Me.

24 "Father, I desire that they also whom You gave Me may be with Me where I am, that they may behold My glory which You have given Me; for You loved Me before the foundation of the world. 25 O righteous Father! The world has not known You, but I have known You; and these have known that You sent Me. 26 And I have declared

to them Your name, and will declare it, that the love with which You loved Me may be in them, and I in them."

---

7. What is the model of unity that Jesus desired His followers to experience in their relationships with one another (see verse 21)?

8. How could Jesus' followers make His invisible love visible to the world (see verse 23)?

REVIEWING THE STORY

In this section of Philippians, the apostle Paul calls for the believers to remain united in love and do nothing out of selfish interests or conceit. He offers up the example of Christ as their model to follow. Although

Jesus was divine, He emptied Himself of power, chose to take the form of a bondservant, and appeared in the likeness of humans. Paul concluded by stressing that one day the universe will acknowledge what the believers in Philippi had come to confess in their worship: "that Jesus Christ is Lord, to the glory of God the Father" (2:11).

9. How does Paul define being "like-minded" (Philippians 2:2)?

_____

_____

_____

_____

_____

_____

_____

_____

_____

10. According to Paul, what should always accompany our self-interest (see Philippians 2:4)?

_____

_____

_____

_____

_____

_____

_____

_____

_____

11. How did Paul describe the mindset of Jesus when He came to earth (see Philippians 2:6–7)?

_____

_____

_____

_____

_____

_____

_____

12. What authority did God give to Christ (see Philippians 2:10–11)?

_____

_____

_____

_____

_____

_____

_____

APPLYING THE MESSAGE

13. How can you guard against selfish ambition and conceit in your own relationships?

_____

_____

_____

_____

_____

14. What can you do to better look after the interests of others?

_____

_____

_____

_____

_____

_____

REFLECTING ON THE MEANING

In this section of Philippians, Paul says to the believers, "If you want to know how to make unity and humility work, just look to the example of Jesus—and do what He did." For Paul, there was no greater example of humility and service than the Lord Jesus Christ. He had worked to model his life after the life of Christ, and he wanted all believers to do the same.

Jesus emphasized unity and humility in His teachings. As He said, "Whoever exalts himself will be humbled, and he who humbles himself will be exalted" (Matthew 23:12). Jesus provided the proof of this promise. He didn't exalt Himself but "humbled Himself and became obedient to the point of death" (Philippians 2:8). As a result, God exalted Him, so that "every knee should bow [and] every tongue should confess that Jesus Christ is Lord" (verses 10–11).

The Bible says that when we exalt ourselves, we drive Jesus away. But when we humble ourselves, He draws near to us. James puts it this way: "Humble yourselves in the sight of the Lord, and He will lift you up" (James 4:10). The apostle Peter says, "Therefore humble yourselves unto the mighty hand of God, that He may exalt you in due time" (1 Peter 5:6).

Our role in creating unity is simply to follow Jesus' example. We are to put the needs of others first in humility just as Christ put our needs first in coming to this world. As we do this, we find that such humility leads to exaltation. The way up is the way down. If the church would ever embrace that concept wholeheartedly, just imagine what unity we would have!

Journaling Your Response

What is the biggest obstacle you face when it comes to humbling yourself?

THE JOY OF RESPONSIBILITY

Philippians 2:12–18

GETTING STARTED

What is the most noteworthy thing you have accomplished in your life through discipline?

_____

_____

_____

_____

_____

_____

_____

_____

_____

_____

SETTING THE STAGE

Paul has just issued a call for the believers in Philippi to model Jesus' humility and look to the interests of others before their own. He has reminded them that Jesus—though He was God—chose to not only take on the flesh of a human being but also appear in the "form of a bondservant" (2:7). Jesus was humble in every way as he followed God's will in His life. This culminated in His ultimate act of service by dying for the sins of humanity on the cross.

Paul begins this next section of his letter with the word, *therefore*. This is a term that tends to get shoved under the rug when we are reading through Scripture, but here it serves as a critical link to what Paul will be discussing next. The apostle wants the believers to keep the example of Jesus in mind as he moves into some practical instruction on how to live. For him, it is not enough to just discuss doctrine with his readers. Rather, he wants them to understand that *doctrine* is a foundation that leads to them taking *action*.

In other words, the apostle Paul is asking the believers to take responsibility for the way they are conducting their lives. Remember, by the time he penned this letter, he was in prison and had been separated from them for some time. So, not only does Paul want them to remember the example that Jesus set for them, but he also wants them to remember the example that he set for them. He reminds them that they had obeyed his teaching when he was present with them. Now that he was absent, it was even more important for them to obey those teachings.

Salvation comes through grace alone—"It is the gift of God, not of works, lest anyone should boast" (Ephesians 2:8–9). But once we accept God's free gift of salvation, we have to take on the responsibility to grow in our faith. Doctrine and teaching are just the foundation. We have to act on what we learn if we want to grow in the Christian life.

EXPLORING THE TEXT

Working Out Salvation (Philippians 2:12–13)

> [12] Therefore, my beloved, as you have always obeyed, not as in my presence only, but now much more in my absence, work out your

own salvation with fear and trembling; [13] for it is God who works in you both to will and to do for His good pleasure.

---

1. How does Paul express his confidence that the believers know how to pursue a godly life? What had they previously demonstrated to him (see verse 12)?

_____

_____

_____

_____

_____

_____

_____

_____

2. Paul was not saying the believers needed to *earn* their salvation (which was impossible) but to live in a way that others saw Jesus in them. This is a huge responsibility! What comfort does Paul offer to those who might feel the weight of this high calling (see verse 13)?

_____

_____

_____

_____

_____

_____

_____

Light Bearers (Philippians 2:14–18)

¹⁴ Do all things without complaining and disputing, ¹⁵ that you may become blameless and harmless, children of God without fault in the midst of a crooked and perverse generation, among whom you shine as lights in the world, ¹⁶ holding fast the word of life, so that I may rejoice in the day of Christ that I have not run in vain or labored in vain.

¹⁷ Yes, and if I am being poured out as a drink offering on the sacrifice and service of your faith, I am glad and rejoice with you all. ¹⁸ For the same reason you also be glad and rejoice with me.

3. The believers in Philippi were living in the midst of a "crooked and perverse generation" and might have had good reason to complain. What does Paul advise them to do instead? What are the benefits of conducting themselves in this manner (see verses 14–16)?

4. In Old Testament times, a drink offering was poured over a sacrifice to God (see Numbers 15:1–10). In what way had Paul served as a "drink offering" to the believers (see 2:17–18)?

_____

_____

_____

_____

_____

_____

_____

_____

_____

_____

GOING DEEPER

In this section of Philippians, Paul draws on the story of the Israelites in the wilderness to show how grumbling and complaining will affect our witness for Christ. The Israelites had been freed from slavery in Egypt, but when times grew difficult, they forgot their blessings and longed to be back with their captors. Paul does not want us to make the same mistake.

Grumbling Against God (Exodus 16:1–3)

¹ And they journeyed from Elim, and all the congregation of the children of Israel came to the Wilderness of Sin, which is between Elim and Sinai, on the fifteenth day of the second month after they departed from the land of Egypt. ² Then the whole congregation of the children of Israel complained against Moses and Aaron in the wilderness. ³ And the children of Israel said to them, "Oh, that we had died by the hand of the LORD in the land of Egypt, when

49

we sat by the pots of meat and when we ate bread to the full! For you have brought us out into this wilderness to kill this whole assembly with hunger."

---

5. The Wilderness of Sin is a desolate wasteland located in the southwestern part of the Sinai Peninsula. What happened when the people entered this place (see verses 2–3)?

_____

_____

_____

_____

_____

_____

_____

_____

6. The Israelites had been delivered from slavery in Egypt barely two months before. What did they remember of their time there (see verse 3)? What does this say about their attitude toward God?

_____

_____

_____

_____

_____

_____

_____

_____

_____

The Israelites Again Complain (Numbers 11:1–6)

¹ Now when the people complained, it displeased the LORD; for the LORD heard it, and His anger was aroused. So the fire of the LORD burned among them, and consumed some in the outskirts of the camp. ² Then the people cried out to Moses, and when Moses prayed to the LORD, the fire was quenched. ³ So he called the name of the place Taberah, because the fire of the LORD had burned among them.

⁴ Now the mixed multitude who were among them yielded to intense craving; so the children of Israel also wept again and said: "Who will give us meat to eat? ⁵ We remember the fish which we ate freely in Egypt, the cucumbers, the melons, the leeks, the onions, and the garlic; ⁶ but now our whole being is dried up; there is nothing at all except this manna before our eyes!"

7. How did the Lord respond to the people's many complaints (see verses 1–3)? What insights does this provide on Paul's instruction for the believers in Philippi to avoid such grumbling so they "may become blameless and harmless" (Philippians 2:15)?

8. What memories did the Israelites again express about their time in Egypt (see verses 4–6)? How did this show a lack of honor and respect to God, their deliverer?

_____

_____

_____

_____

_____

_____

_____

REVIEWING THE STORY

The apostle Paul encouraged the believers in Philippi to embrace the joy of responsibility. He reminds them that his time on this earth is drawing to a close and that he likely will not be with them again. For this reason, they needed to "work out" their own salvation as God directed them. Furthermore, they were to serve God without grumbling and complaining, so they might shine as examples for Christ in the world. Paul states that if they do these things, he will rejoice in the sacrifice he made on their behalf—knowing that his work among them has been fruitful.

9. What was the legacy of the Philippian believers (see Philippians 2:12)?

_____

_____

_____

_____

_____

_____

_____

10. For what purpose does Paul say that God works in us (see Philippians 2:13)?

_____

_____

_____

_____

_____

_____

_____

11. What happens when believers do "all things without complaining and disputing" (Philippians 2:14–15)?

_____

_____

_____

_____

_____

_____

_____

12. What reasons does Paul give for being able to rejoice in the day of Christ if the Philippian believers held "fast the word of life" (Philippians 2:16)?

_____

_____

_____

_____

_____

_____

APPLYING THE MESSAGE

13. What practical steps are you taking to "work out" your own salvation in your life?

_____

_____

_____

_____

_____

_____

_____

_____

_____

_____

_____

_____

14. What helps you to walk through life without grumbling or complaining?

_____

_____

_____

_____

_____

_____

_____

_____

_____

_____

_____

_____

REFLECTING ON THE MEANING

The apostle Paul begins this section of his letter with the instruction, "My beloved . . . work out your own salvation with fear and trembling" (2:12). It is important to note that when Paul issues this command, he is not advising them to work *for* their salvation. Rather, the phrase "work out" has the meaning of working *through* something to its full completion.

This expression was used in Paul's day to describe those who worked in the mines. The miners "worked out" the treasures in the ground that had been placed there by the Creator. In the same way, believers in Christ are to "work out" the treasures in their lives that have already been placed there by their Redeemer. They are to work out what God has "worked in." As Paul continues, we discover that there are two practical ways to accomplish this work.

First, we take the responsibility to do our part. Paul and the other New Testament writers were unanimous in their assertion that salvation comes not as a result of any human effort but solely through the grace of God. However, in many of these passages where the doctrine of salvation *apart from works* is found, the doctrine of salvation *unto good works* can also be found. Just consider these words from Paul to the Ephesians: "For by grace you have been saved through faith, and that not of yourselves. . . . For we are His workmanship, created in Christ Jesus for good works, which God prepared beforehand" (2:8–10).

Second, we depend on God to do His part. Paul writes, "It is God who works in you both to will and to do for His good pleasure" (Philippians 2:13). As believers in Christ, we work out our salvation, knowing that God has already been at work within us. Just like the workers in the mine, we are at work to pull out the treasures that He has already placed within our lives. Both divine enablement and human responsibility are involved in the process of growing our faith.

The Lord will not do for us what we should be doing ourselves. But as we cooperate in partnership with Him, we will see the potential of our Christian lives realized.

Journaling Your Response

What do you sense today that God is instructing you to do?

THE JOY OF MINISTRY

Philippians 2:19–30

GETTING STARTED

How has someone served to be a role model in your life?

_____

_____

_____

_____

_____

_____

_____

_____

_____

_____

_____

_____

_____

_____

_____

_____

_____

_____

_____

_____

_____

SETTING THE STAGE

Role models come in all shapes and sizes—and from all different backgrounds and walks of life. The people we choose to serve as our role models say a lot about us, what inspires us, what we consider to be important, and who we aspire to be. The right role models can have a profound effect on our lives. They can give us direction and encouragement in our walk with Christ.

Paul has just instructed the believers in Philippi to look to Jesus as their ultimate role model. As he wrote, "Let this mind be in you which was also in Christ Jesus, who, being in the form of God, did not consider it robbery to be equal with God, but made Himself of no reputation, taking the form of a bondservant, and coming in the likeness of men" (2:5–7). The believers were to especially imitate Christ in their humility and service to one another.

In this next section, Paul identifies two other role models for the believers' consideration—two individuals who illustrate what it means to have the mind of Christ. The first is Timothy, his coworker and protégé. Paul had met Timothy in Lystra during his second missionary journey. He was well respected in the community, and Paul and Silas had taken him along on their travels. Since that time, Timothy had proven to be a model of service in his concern for others, his consecration to the Lord, and his commitment to the gospel.

The second person whom Paul names is Epaphroditus. The believers in Philippi knew this individual well, for he was the delegate they sent to deliver the financial gift to Paul while he was in prison. Epaphroditus had worked so tirelessly in aiding and serving Paul that he had fallen ill and almost died. But he recovered, and now Paul was not only sending him back to Philippi, but he was also holding him up as a model of godliness in the midst of suffering.

These two men—in addition to the apostle Paul himself—serve as models to us as well of what it means to love others and experience true joy through ministry.

EXPLORING THE TEXT

Timothy Commended (Philippians 2:19–24)

¹⁹ But I trust in the Lord Jesus to send Timothy to you shortly, that I also may be encouraged when I know your state. ²⁰ For I have no one like-minded, who will sincerely care for your state. ²¹ For all seek their own, not the things which are of Christ Jesus. ²² But you know his proven character, that as a son with his father he served with me in the gospel. ²³ Therefore I hope to send him at once, as soon as I see how it goes with me. ²⁴ But I trust in the Lord that I myself shall also come shortly.

1. Paul tells the Philippians that he is planning on sending Timothy back to them . . . though not right away. Why does he eventually want to send Timothy? What set him apart from others who had ministered in the Philippian church (see verses 19–21)?

2. Compare this passage with 1 Thessalonians 3:2–3 and 1 Corinthians 4:17. How did Paul view Timothy? What role did he serve in Paul's ministry (Philippians 2:22–23)?

_____

_____

_____

_____

_____

_____

_____

_____

_____

_____

_____

_____

_____

Epaphroditus Praised (Philippians 2:25–30)

25 Yet I considered it necessary to send to you Epaphroditus, my brother, fellow worker, and fellow soldier, but your messenger and the one who ministered to my need; 26 since he was longing for you all, and was distressed because you had heard that he was sick. 27 For indeed he was sick almost unto death; but God had mercy on him, and not only on him but on me also, lest I should have sorrow upon sorrow. 28 Therefore I sent him the more eagerly, that when you see him again you may rejoice, and I may be less sorrowful. 29 Receive him therefore in the Lord with all gladness, and hold such men in esteem; 30 because for the work of Christ he came close to death, not regarding his life, to supply what was lacking in your service toward me.

3. The believers had sent Epaphroditus to deliver a monetary gift and stay with Paul to minister to his needs. Why was Paul sending him back so soon? What characteristics made Epaphroditus such a valuable coworker for Paul (see verses 25–27)?

_____

_____

_____

_____

_____

_____

_____

_____

_____

_____

_____

4. How had Epaphroditus proved himself in his service to Paul? What sacrifice was Paul making in sending this trusted worker back to Philippi (see verses 28–30)?

_____

_____

_____

_____

_____

_____

_____

_____

_____

Going Deeper

Little is known about Epaphroditus outside these passages in Philippians. However, Paul mentions Timothy throughout his letters—and writes two personal letters to him—and Luke records several stories in Acts involving Timothy and his work in Paul's ministry. The following account explains how Paul first met Timothy and decided to take him on his journeys.

Timothy Joins Paul and Silas (Acts 16:1–5)

[1] Then he came to Derbe and Lystra. And behold, a certain disciple was there, named Timothy, the son of a certain Jewish woman who believed, but his father was Greek. [2] He was well spoken of by the brethren who were at Lystra and Iconium. [3] Paul wanted to have him go on with him. And he took him and circumcised him because of the Jews who were in that region, for they all knew that his father was Greek. [4] And as they went through the cities, they delivered to them the decrees to keep, which were determined by the apostles and elders at Jerusalem. [5] So the churches were strengthened in the faith, and increased in number daily.

5. How does Luke describe Timothy's mixed heritage in this passage? How was Timothy regarded among the members of the community in Lystra (see verses 1–2)?

_____

_____

_____

_____

_____

_____

_____

6. Timothy, being the son of a Greek Gentile, had not been circumcised. Why would this have been a problem in Paul's ministry to the Jews? What was the purpose (see verses 3–5)?

_____

_____

_____

_____

_____

_____

_____

_____

Paul told the Philippians that Timothy had served "as a son with his father" in the work of sharing the gospel (see 2:22). Since the time of their first meeting in Lystra, he had continued to serve alongside Paul, ministering to the young churches and co-authoring many of the apostle's letters. In the following passage, Paul provides some additional details about Timothy's work and character—traits that made him an effective role model in ministry.

Take Heed to Your Ministry (1 Timothy 4:12–16)

¹² Let no one despise your youth, but be an example to the believers in word, in conduct, in love, in spirit, in faith, in purity. ¹³ Till I come, give attention to reading, to exhortation, to doctrine. ¹⁴ Do not neglect the gift that is in you, which was given to you by prophecy with the laying on of the hands of the eldership. ¹⁵ Meditate on these things; give yourself entirely to them, that your progress may be evident to all. ¹⁶ Take heed to yourself and to the doctrine. Continue in them, for in doing this you will save both yourself and those who hear you.

7. In Paul's day, respected teachers were generally individuals more than forty years old who had gained a lot of life experience. But scholars believe that Timothy might have been in his *thirties* when he began pastoring the church in Ephesus. How does Paul advise Timothy to counter this possible bias against him (see verses 12–13)?

_____

_____

_____

_____

_____

_____

_____

_____

_____

8. What does Paul say about Timothy's gifts? How does he encourage Timothy to lead his congregation (see verses 14–16)?

_____

_____

_____

_____

_____

_____

_____

_____

_____

REVIEWING THE STORY

The apostle Paul helped the believers recognize the joy of ministry by commending two people who had excelled in their service. The first was

Timothy, his coworker whom he commended for his character and work in sharing the gospel. Paul hoped to send Timothy back to Philippi soon, once the situation regarding his imprisonment had been resolved. The second individual was Epaphroditus, who had been sent as a delegate from Philippi and had fallen ill. Paul wanted the believers to know that he had recovered and was coming back to them soon.

9. Why did Paul want to send Timothy back to Philippi (see Philippians 2:19)?

_____

_____

_____

_____

_____

_____

_____

_____

10. What did the Philippian believers know of Timothy (see Philippians 2:22)?

_____

_____

_____

_____

_____

_____

_____

11. Why did Paul consider it necessary to send Epaphroditus to the church in Philippi (see Philippians 2:26)?

_____

_____

_____

_____

_____

_____

12. Why did Paul instruct the Philippian believers to hold individuals such as Epaphroditus in high esteem (see Philippians 2:29–30)?

_____

_____

_____

_____

_____

_____

_____

APPLYING THE MESSAGE

13. How are you serving as a role model in other people's lives?

_____

_____

_____

_____

_____

_____

14. How are you finding joy in your ministry to others?

_____

_____

_____

_____

_____

_____

_____

REFLECTING ON THE MEANING

Whether we realize it or not, each of us is a role model to someone else. No matter who we are, people are watching us, paying attention to us, and taking cues from how we live. This means that what we do *matters*. We may not be eager to embrace such a role, or feel ready to accept the responsibility, but that won't stop people from following our example.

Paul recognized Timothy and Epaphroditus in this section because he felt that these two men were serving as effective role models in how to serve Christ. Elsewhere, Paul offered up himself as such a role model. While at first glance this may seem self-serving, this was not done out of pride but because he had worked hard to model the selflessness and discipline that he wanted his readers to embrace. He had no illusions about his own goodness, apart from Christ. This is why he wrote, "Imitate me, just as I also imitate Christ" (1 Corinthians 11:1).

As believers in Christ, we need to recognize that we have a decisive role in the lives of people around us—our families, neighbors, coworkers, and acquaintances. We can model Jesus Christ to them, just as Timothy, Epaphroditus, and Paul modeled Christ to the people of their day. Therefore, our prayer needs to be, "Lord God, help me to be the person You want me to be so that when others see me, they will be drawn to You."

God has given you the Holy Spirit to help you accomplish this goal. So each day, give your life over to Him. Each morning, say to Him, "Holy

Spirit, control my life today. Help me model Christ today." He will hear your prayer and help you be the person God wants you to be . . . so that when people see you, they see Christ.

JOURNALING YOUR RESPONSE

How do you respond to the idea that someone looks to you as a role model?

THE JOY OF HUMILITY

Philippians 3:1–11

GETTING STARTED

Why is it so difficult to be truly humble?

_____

_____

_____

_____

_____

_____

_____

_____

_____

_____

_____

_____

_____

_____

SETTING THE STAGE

Several times during his ministry, Paul was put in the uncomfortable position of having to defend his integrity, his motives, and his character in the work that he was doing among his churches. We can often sense his discomfort in those passages when he is forced to make such a defense. From the moment of his encounter with Christ, he had embraced a spirit of humility. He wanted to be known only as "Paul, a bondservant of Jesus Christ" (Romans 1:1).

However, the accusations leveled against him by false teachers often required him to explain his intentions and reveal details about his background. We come to one of these circumstances in the next section of his letter to the Philippians. The problem arose out of the fact that Paul—being in prison—was unable to visit the believers. In his absence, false teachers had infiltrated the church and were preaching a gospel that was based on works. They were trying to convince the believers in Philippi that to be Christians, they first had to convert to Judaism. Specifically, in this instance, they were saying that practice of *circumcision* was necessary for salvation.

Paul recognized that he was uniquely qualified to expose the dangerous fallacy behind this teaching. After all, if ever there were such a thing as a "true Jew," he would have been placed in the very top percentile. His credentials were impeccable. His birth, his pedigree, his education, his social standing, his understanding of Mosaic law, and his zeal for Judaism had all set him apart from his Jewish contemporaries.

In other words, if salvation could have been earned through credentials alone . . . Paul would have earned it. Yet he knew better than anyone that his credentials were useless as a means of salvation. So, in this section of his letter, he boasts just enough about his Jewish credentials to help the believers understand how little those credentials meant.

EXPLORING THE TEXT

Rejoice in the Lord (Philippians 3:1–6)

¹ Finally, my brethren, rejoice in the Lord. For me to write the same things to you is not tedious, but for you it is safe.

² Beware of dogs, beware of evil workers, beware of the muti-lation! ³ For we are the circumcision, who worship God in the Spirit, rejoice in Christ Jesus, and have no confidence in the flesh, ⁴ though I also might have confidence in the flesh. If anyone else thinks he may have confidence in the flesh, I more so: ⁵ circumcised the eighth day, of the stock of Israel, of the tribe of Benjamin, a Hebrew of the Hebrews; concerning the law, a Pharisee; ⁶ concerning zeal, persecuting the church; concerning the righteousness which is in the law, blameless.

---

1. Paul's note that it is "not tedious" for him to "write the same things" likely means he was going to share something with the believers that he already told them. In this case, he is warning them again about false teachers who were preaching that Gentiles had to be circumcised (to "become Jewish") before they could receive salvation. How does Paul view these individuals? How does he respond to their claims (see verses 1–3)?

2. These teachers had "confidence in the flesh" and believed that strict keeping of the law was necessary for salvation. How does Paul combat this argument by offering up the example of his own life? Why was he uniquely qualified to speak on this subject (see verses 4–6)?

All for Christ (Philippians 3:7–11)

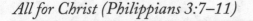

[7] But what things were gain to me, these I have counted loss for Christ. [8] Yet indeed I also count all things loss for the excellence of the knowledge of Christ Jesus my Lord, for whom I have suffered the loss of all things, and count them as rubbish, that I may gain Christ [9] and be found in Him, not having my own righteousness, which is from the law, but that which is through faith in Christ, the righteousness which is from God by faith; [10] that I may know Him and the power of His resurrection, and the fellowship of His sufferings, being conformed to His death, [11] if, by any means, I may attain to the resurrection from the dead.

3. Paul once believed that his privileged Jewish status gave him special standing before God. What did he discover was the truth about this "special status" (see verses 7–9)?

_____

_____

_____

_____

_____

_____

4. Paul had lost much in following Christ—including his status, his reputation, and even his security. What only did he wish to attain now (see verses 10–11)?

_____

_____

_____

_____

_____

_____

GOING DEEPER

Paul's encounter with Christ had taught him that no amount of religious rule-keeping could secure his salvation. It was only by God's grace that he had been saved—"The gift of God, not of works, lest anyone should boast" (Ephesians 2:8–9). This realization had led Paul to minister and serve other believers with humility. In doing so, Paul was modeling the actions of his Lord and Savior, Jesus Christ, as the following story told in the Gospel of John demonstrates.

Jesus Washes the Disciples' Feet (John 13:1–9)

¹ Now before the Feast of the Passover, when Jesus knew that His hour had come that He should depart from this world to the Father, having loved His own who were in the world, He loved them to the end.

² And supper being ended, the devil having already put it into the heart of Judas Iscariot, Simon's son, to betray Him, ³ Jesus, knowing that the Father had given all things into His hands, and that He had come from God and was going to God, ⁴ rose from supper and laid aside His garments, took a towel and girded Himself. ⁵ After that, He poured water into a basin and began to wash the disciples' feet, and to wipe them with the towel with which He was girded. ⁶ Then He came to Simon Peter. And Peter said to Him, "Lord, are You washing my feet?"

⁷ Jesus answered and said to him, "What I am doing you do not understand now, but you will know after this."

⁸ Peter said to Him, "You shall never wash my feet!"

Jesus answered him, "If I do not wash you, you have no part with Me."

⁹ Simon Peter said to Him, "Lord, not my feet only, but also my hands and my head!"

---

5. John relates how Jesus—God Himself in human form—willingly embraced the role of a servant by washing the dirty feet of His disciples. How did this action demonstrate His humility? How did the disciple Peter react to this action (see verses 3–6)?

---

6. How did Jesus respond to Peter's outburst? What do you think Jesus meant when He said that if He did not wash Peter's feet, the disciple would have no part with Him (see verses 7–8)?

_____

_____

_____

_____

_____

_____

_____

_____

_____

_____

_____

A Servant Is Not Greater Than His Master (John 13:10–17)

[10] Jesus said to him, "He who is bathed needs only to wash his feet, but is completely clean; and you are clean, but not all of you." [11] For He knew who would betray Him; therefore He said, "You are not all clean."

[12] So when He had washed their feet, taken His garments, and sat down again, He said to them, "Do you know what I have done to you? [13] You call Me Teacher and Lord, and you say well, for so I am. [14] If I then, your Lord and Teacher, have washed your feet, you also ought to wash one another's feet. [15] For I have given you an example, that you should do as I have done to you. [16] Most assuredly, I say to you, a servant is not greater than his master; nor is he who is sent greater than he who sent him. [17] If you know these things, blessed are you if you do them.

7. What did Jesus indicate was the point of His washing the disciples' feet (see verses 12–15)?

_____

_____

_____

_____

_____

_____

8. Jesus reminds us that "a servant is not greater than his master." How should this impact our feelings that some act of service is "beneath us" to do? What are we really saying when we choose *not* to serve others (see verses 16–17)?

_____

_____

_____

_____

_____

REVIEWING THE STORY

Paul warns the believers in Philippi to watch out for anyone who teaches they must first become Jewish in order to become Christians. He speaks against these false teachers who "have confidence in the flesh" (3:4), stating that if anyone had reason to be confident in their Jewish heritage and rule keeping . . . it was him. He was religious, zealous, and strict in his adherence to the law, but after meeting Christ, he realized that none of that mattered. Now, Paul only wanted to model the humble service of his Lord and Savior and continue his work of sharing the message of salvation to the world.

9. How did Paul refer to the false teachers who had infiltrated the Philippian church in his absence (see Philippians 3:2)?

10. How did the apostle Paul summarize his Christian credentials (see Philippians 3:5)?

11. Why did Paul suffer the loss of all things and count them as rubbish (see Philippians 3:8)?

12. What important point does Paul make about righteousness (see Philippians 3:9)?

_____

_____

_____

_____

_____

_____

_____

APPLYING THE MESSAGE

13. What are some ways you have fallen into the trap of thinking you have to earn God's favor?

_____

_____

_____

_____

_____

_____

_____

14. How does the example of Jesus' humility compel you to serve others?

_____

_____

_____

_____

_____

_____

_____

REFLECTING ON THE MEANING

The apostle Paul counted everything that he had gained in his former life as a Pharisee—all the honor, prestige, and security it brought—as "loss" and "rubbish" as compared to the knowledge he had gained through Christ. Meeting Jesus had forever changed his priorities, goals, and values. In this section, he outlines what he now only wants to know about Christ.

First, *he wanted to know the person of Jesus Christ*. Many Christians have knowledge of Christ . . . but it is just *head* knowledge rather than *heart* knowledge. It is not enough for us to just know *about* Jesus and subscribe to His agenda. When we become Christians, we enter into a relationship with the Son of the living God, and we must deepen that relationship. We do this through worship, prayer, Bible study, and by following Jesus' example—demonstrating kindness, humility, and forgiveness to others as we cultivate a thankful attitude.

Second, *Paul wants to know the power of Christ and His resurrection*. As believers, we experienced the power of Christ at our salvation. But Paul states that as we go through life, this same power is available to us in our times of need. The question we must ask is whether we have ever *accessed* that power. Sometimes this requires taking steps of faith that seem beyond our present capability. Yet as we walk by faith, God shows us that He is able to do above and beyond all that we will ever ask or think. Paul wanted to see this kind of power in his life.

Third, *Paul wants to know the passion of Christ and the fellowship of His sufferings*. The apostle was actually praying for the opportunity to identify with Christ in His suffering! He understood his sufferings united him with the Lord in a way unlike any other. Likewise, the suffering we endure can bring us into the realm of the suffering the Lord Jesus went through on the cross. We can come to know Jesus more closely during such times.

As Jesus said, "Blessed are you when they revile and persecute you, and say all kinds of evil against you falsely for My sake. Rejoice and be exceedingly glad, for great is your reward in heaven, for so they persecuted the prophets who were before you" (Matthew 5:11–12).

JOURNALING YOUR RESPONSE

What are some ways that you are seeking to know Christ better each day?

THE JOY OF VICTORY

Philippians 3:12–16

GETTING STARTED

What is one recent goal in your life that you had success in attaining?

_____

_____

_____

_____

_____

_____

_____

_____

_____

_____

_____

_____

_____

_____

_____

_____

_____

SETTING THE STAGE

All good coaches have a "philosophy on winning" that they work to instill in their players. For John Wooden, one of the greatest sports coaches to ever live, this philosophy boiled down to three key principles: (1) conditioning, (2) fundamentals, and (3) teamwork. Wooden wanted his players to be properly *conditioned* so they would still have stamina late in the game. He drilled his players on the *fundamentals* so they could perform under pressure. He encouraged *teamwork* so the players would function as a unit and achieve more victories.

In many ways, Paul sought to instill these traits in the lives of his "players." He wanted the believers in Philippi to understand the Christian life is like running a marathon that requires *conditioning* and perseverance. He wanted them to know the *fundamentals* of the Christian faith so they would not be duped by false teachers. He wanted them to function as a *team* so they could accomplish more together than they would working on their own.

What is surprising about Paul's formula on winning is that he wrote it from a prison cell in Rome. Based on outward appearances, the apostle had lost his race—his freedom, his fellowship with his churches, and likely his very life. But Paul understood that victory is not based on present circumstances. He was looking toward a greater goal—toward a greater *prize*—that he wanted to attain. He was focused not on his present trials as a citizen of earth but on the future rewards that awaited him as a citizen of heaven.

Like Coach Wooden, the apostle Paul lived out this philosophy every day. He tirelessly worked to impress these principles in the lives of believers. He strove to keep them focused on the prize so they could secure the path to victory. As a result, he became one of the greatest coaches the world has ever seen on living a victorious life in Christ.

EXPLORING THE TEXT

Press Toward the Goal (Philippians 3:12–14)

---

[12] Not that I have already attained, or am already perfected; but I press on, that I may lay hold of that for which Christ Jesus has also laid hold of me. [13] Brethren, I do not count myself to have apprehended; but one thing I do, forgetting those things which are behind and reaching

forward to those things which are ahead, ¹⁴ I press toward the goal for the prize of the upward call of God in Christ Jesus.

---

1. It is possible that Paul's previous teaching on the things he has gained in Christ caused him to worry his readers would think he had attained some sort of "spiritual perfection." How does he let the Philippians know in this passage this is not the case (see verse 12)?

_____

_____

_____

_____

2. Runners know that a backward glance at ground already covered will only slow their progress toward the finish. How does Paul employ this imagery in describing the "race" that he is running? What was he encouraging the Philippians to likewise do (see verses 13–14)?

_____

_____

_____

_____

Be of the Same Mind (Philippians 3:15–16)

¹⁵ Therefore let us, as many as are mature, have this mind; and if in anything you think otherwise, God will reveal even this to you. ¹⁶ Nevertheless, to the degree that we have already attained, let us walk by the same rule, let us be of the same mind.

---

3. Paul has been deliberate in stating that he is still "running the race." What does he say will happen to those who believe they have achieved all the spiritual maturity they need—or those who see no need to continue pressing toward the ultimate goal (see verse 15)?

_____

_____

_____

_____

_____

4. Paul's statement, "walk by the same rule," refers to soldiers marching in formation. What qualities of soldiers did Paul want to see in the way the believers lived (see verse 16)?

_____

_____

_____

_____

GOING DEEPER

The imagery of a runner would have been familiar to Paul's readers in Philippi and elsewhere in Greece. The history of running in the region can be traced back as far as 776 BC, and by the time of Paul, events were held regularly in all the Greek cities. Perhaps this is why Paul also uses this imagery of a runner to describe the Christian race in his first letter to the Corinthians.

Striving for a Crown (1 Corinthians 9:24–27)

24 Do you not know that those who run in a race all run, but one receives the prize? Run in such a way that you may obtain it. 25 And everyone who competes for the prize is temperate in all things. Now

they do it to obtain a perishable crown, but we for an imperishable crown. [26] Therefore I run thus: not with uncertainty. Thus I fight: not as one who beats the air. [27] But I discipline my body and bring it into subjection, lest, when I have preached to others, I myself should become disqualified.

---

5. How does Paul describe the goal of a runner in a race? How are the believers to run their "race" in living for Christ (see verses 24–25)?

_____

_____

_____

_____

_____

_____

6. What does Paul say about the way he "conditions" himself for the race (see verses 26–27)? What similarities do you see between Paul's words to the Corinthians and the Philippians?

_____

_____

_____

_____

_____

_____

History reveals that Paul ran his race for Christ . . . and ran it well all the days of his life on earth. Scholars tell us that Paul's second letter to his co-worker Timothy was likely written shortly before the apostle's death. In the pages of this letter, he reflects on his own Christian journey. At long last, he was able to claim victory in the name of Jesus Christ his Savior.

Preach the Word (2 Timothy 4:1–8)

¹ I charge you therefore before God and the Lord Jesus Christ, who will judge the living and the dead at His appearing and His kingdom: ² Preach the word! Be ready in season and out of season. Convince, rebuke, exhort, with all longsuffering and teaching. ³ For the time will come when they will not endure sound doctrine, but according to their own desires, because they have itching ears, they will heap up for themselves teachers; ⁴ and they will turn their ears away from the truth, and be turned aside to fables. ⁵ But you be watchful in all things, endure afflictions, do the work of an evangelist, fulfill your ministry.

⁶ For I am already being poured out as a drink offering, and the time of my departure is at hand. ⁷ I have fought the good fight, I have finished the race, I have kept the faith. ⁸ Finally, there is laid up for me the crown of righteousness, which the Lord, the righteous Judge, will give to me on that Day, and not to me only but also to all who have loved His appearing.

7. Paul knew he was nearing the end of his "race" and wanted to issue some final instructions to Timothy. What did he want Timothy to do? What was the urgency that he felt in making this request to his young protégé (see verses 1–4)?

8. As previously noted, in Old Testament times a drink offering was poured over a sacrifice to God. In what way was Paul being poured out as a drink offering (see verses 6–8)?

_____

_____

_____

_____

_____

_____

_____

REVIEWING THE STORY

The apostle Paul is careful to point out in this section of Philippians that he has not attained any form of "spiritual perfection." Rather, he compares himself to a runner in a race who is pressing on to reach the goal. He knows that looking at his past life and mistakes will serve no purpose in the race he is running, so he seeks to put those things behind him and stay focused on the finish line. He warns those who believe they have attained some level of spiritual maturity to stay in the race. He concludes by asking the believers to be one in mind with him on this point.

9. Why did Paul continue to press on in his race (see Philippians 3:12)?

_____

_____

_____

_____

_____

_____

_____

10. What is the "one thing" that Paul did in his race (Philippians 3:13)?

11. How do mature believers become aware of any incorrect thinking (see Philippians 3:15)?

12. What were Paul's instructions to the mature believers in Philippi (see Philippians 3:16)?

APPLYING THE MESSAGE

13. What does victory in Christ look like in your life?

14. How do you stay focused on the "prize" as you run your race?

_____

_____

_____

_____

REFLECTING ON THE MEANING

In this section of Philippians, the apostle Paul uses athletic imagery to describe his approach to the Christian life. The phrase "reaching forward" describes a runner in a foot race who stretches out to cross the finish line first (see verses 12–13). However, Paul notes he has not yet *apprehended* or *attained* this goal. Paul is still "running the race."

Paul is basically saying, "I am at the zenith of my life. I have founded churches. I have led countless people to Christ. I have maintained my faith through the worst of circumstances. But I don't consider myself as having arrived." Instead of being proud of what he has accomplished, he is still pushing forward. Likewise, realizing we have not yet arrived in our race will keep us focused on reaching the goal. We have not yet achieved perfection in our effort to be like Christ. We still have room to grow.

Paul also uses the phrase, "I press toward the goal" (verse 14). As runners reach the end of a long-distance race, they are virtually spent. The veins in their neck bulge. The tension in their body is apparent. This is the image Paul presents regarding his Christian race. He did not treat his spiritual growth in a casual way. He didn't say, "If I get around to it, I'm going to try to develop my spiritual life a little bit this week." No, it was his focus and his drive. He was seeking the prize—the crown of righteousness—that God gives to those who walk with Him.

As Christians, our goal, vision, and drive should be to follow the example that Paul set for us so we can be more like Christ and serve Him with all of our hearts. Jesus desires for us to become like Him. He wants us to grow in our faith and develop the godly qualities we find in

Scripture. If we want to know Christ and grow in Him, we need to get serious about it. We need to carve out time to make it happen so we can experience true victory in Christ.

JOURNALING YOUR RESPONSE

What does pressing toward the goal look like in your life?

THE JOY OF MATURITY

Philippians 3:17–21

GETTING STARTED

What are the telltale signs of someone who is spiritually mature?

_____

_____

_____

_____

_____

_____

_____

_____

_____

_____

_____

_____

_____

_____

_____

SETTING THE STAGE

In recent years, psychologists have coined the phrase "Peter Pan Syndrome" to refer to the difficultly that some young people have in making the transition from adolescence to adulthood. The syndrome manifests in a variety of ways: a delay in moving out of their parents' house, a lack of interest in dating, or an overwhelming fondness for the things of childhood. It is, in a sense, a refusal to take responsibility for one's own adult life.

In this next section of Philippians, the apostle Paul points out a kind of "Peter Pan Syndrome" that was happening in some of the believers' spiritual lives. This phenomenon was not just occurring in Philippi, but in other congregations where Paul had ministered. The believers had put their trust in Christ, received the assurance of eternal life . . . and then stopped growing. They were "babes in Christ" and content to nourish themselves on spiritual "milk and not with solid food" (1 Corinthians 3:2–3).

The Peter Pan Syndrome is still prevalent today. Many believers are grateful that God has saved them from their sin. They are excited about the prospect of spending eternity with God in heaven. But this is the extent of their Christian life. Spiritually speaking, they are stuck in childhood. They haven't stopped to consider that God expects them to grow and mature. They do not realize they could—and *should*—be nourishing themselves on solid spiritual food.

While it is easy to point fingers at others, most believers will admit they have not matured spiritually as quickly as they had hoped. Most of us still experience moments of alarming immaturity in our walk with Christ. Paul's words in this section of Philippians remind us to keep pressing on and moving ahead in running our Christian race.

EXPLORING THE TEXT

Follow Paul's Example (Philippians 3:17–19)

---

17 Brethren, join in following my example, and note those who so walk, as you have us for a pattern. 18 For many walk, of whom I have told you often, and now tell you even weeping, that they are the enemies of the cross of Christ: 19 whose end is destruction, whose

god is their belly, and whose glory is in their shame—who set their mind on earthly things.

---

1. Paul had previously held up Timothy and Epaphroditus as role models for believers. Here he adds his own situation as an example. What advantage did the Philippian believers enjoy because of their association with these three men (see verse 17)?

_____

_____

_____

_____

_____

2. Paul mentions "the enemies of the cross of Christ," who in this case were not pagans but people who identified as Christians—fellow members of the Philippian church. How were they making their spiritual immaturity apparent (see verses 18–19)?

_____

_____

_____

_____

Our Citizenship Is in Heaven (Philippians 3:20–21)

20 For our citizenship is in heaven, from which we also eagerly wait for the Savior, the Lord Jesus Christ, 21 who will transform our lowly body that it may be conformed to His glorious body, according to the working by which He is able even to subdue all things to Himself.

---

3. Philippi was an outpost of Rome for the Romans, just as earth is an outpost of heaven for believers. How would that image have helped the Philippians, who knew what it was like to live in an outpost, understand that they belonged to a different country (see verse 20)?

_____

_____

_____

_____

_____

4. Paul reminds the believers of the goal of their spiritual maturity: the future resurrection of their bodies (see verse 21). How might this have compelled them to press on?

_____

_____

_____

_____

Going Deeper

It is likely that a situation in Corinth was fresh on Paul's mind when he penned these words to the Philippians. In that congregation, the believers' spiritual immaturity had caused them to splinter, with different groups prioritizing allegiance to different leaders. In the following passage, Paul helps them understand the people they were revering were all fellow workers in the gospel. They needed to grow up, quit bickering among themselves, and start working toward the same goal of reaching spiritual maturity in Christ.

Babes in Christ (1 Corinthians 3:1–8)

¹ And I, brethren, could not speak to you as to spiritual people but as to carnal, as to babes in Christ. ² I fed you with milk and not with

solid food; for until now you were not able to receive it, and even now you are still not able; ³ for you are still carnal. For where there are envy, strife, and divisions among you, are you not carnal and behaving like mere men? ⁴ For when one says, "I am of Paul," and another, "I am of Apollos," are you not carnal?

⁵ Who then is Paul, and who is Apollos, but ministers through whom you believed, as the Lord gave to each one? ⁶ I planted, Apollos watered, but God gave the increase. ⁷ So then neither he who plants is anything, nor he who waters, but God who gives the increase. ⁸ Now he who plants and he who waters are one, and each one will receive his own reward according to his own labor.

---

5. A "carnal" person, in this context, is a spiritually immature believer. How had Paul tried to help the believers in Corinth become more spiritually mature? What evidence made Paul realize the believers were still carnal (see verses 1–4)?

_____

_____

_____

_____

_____

6. What do Paul's words concerning himself and Apollos teach about the dangers of placing Christian leaders on a pedestal (see verses 5–8)?

_____

_____

_____

_____

_____

_____

Watering, Working, Warning (1 Corinthians 3:9–17)

⁹ For we are God's fellow workers; you are God's field, you are God's building. ¹⁰ According to the grace of God which was given to me, as a wise master builder I have laid the foundation, and another builds on it. But let each one take heed how he builds on it. ¹¹ For no other foundation can anyone lay than that which is laid, which is Jesus Christ. ¹² Now if anyone builds on this foundation with gold, silver, precious stones, wood, hay, straw, ¹³ each one's work will become clear; for the Day will declare it, because it will be revealed by fire; and the fire will test each one's work, of what sort it is. ¹⁴ If anyone's work which he has built on it endures, he will receive a reward. ¹⁵ If anyone's work is burned, he will suffer loss; but he himself will be saved, yet so as through fire.

¹⁶ Do you not know that you are the temple of God and that the Spirit of God dwells in you? ¹⁷ If anyone defiles the temple of God, God will destroy him. For the temple of God is holy, which temple you are.

7. Paul knew it was important for the believers in Corinth to become spiritually mature if the church was to survive. They needed to discern false teachings that infiltrated the church and raise up younger believers in the faith. How does Paul describe this process of "laying the foundation" that needed to take place (see verses 11–15)?

_____

_____

_____

_____

_____

_____

_____

8. The word *temple* refers to the sacred inner chamber where God dwelled among His people. Here Paul uses it to refer to the church. What warning does Paul issue to people who create divisions in or disrupt the ministry of the church (see verses 16–17)?

_____

_____

_____

_____

_____

REVIEWING THE STORY

Paul calls the believers to follow his example, and that of Timothy and Epaphroditus, in pressing on in their faith. He reminds them of believers who started out strong, but because they never matured in their faith, are now "enemies of the cross of Christ" (3:18). Such individuals set their mind on earthly things and did not disengage from the ways of the world. Paul urges the believers to remember their citizenship is in heaven, to wait for the return of their Lord, and to look forward to the day of their resurrection.

9. How did Paul describe the "end" for the enemies of the cross (see Philippians 3:19)?

_____

_____

_____

_____

10. What god do the enemies of the cross of Christ serve (see Philippians 3:19)?

_____

_____

_____

_____

11. How should Christians view their citizenship (see Philippians 3:20)?

12. For what purpose will the Lord transform our lowly physical bodies (Philippians 3:21)?

APPLYING THE MESSAGE

13. What evidence of spiritual maturity do you see in your life?

14. In what areas do you need to become more mature in your walk with Christ?

_____

_____

_____

_____

_____

REFLECTING ON THE MEANING

One of the products of Paul's spiritual maturity was his ability to encourage those around him. He held the standards of the faith high, and he found ways to inspire his followers to continue to strive toward the upward calling of the Lord Jesus Christ. In this section of Philippians, he identifies two groups of people: those with "this mind," and those who "think otherwise" (Philippians 3:15).

The people of "this mind" are those who have decided growth and maturity are important goals. They acknowledge they need to keep pressing toward the mark of spiritual maturity. Those who "think otherwise" assume they have already arrived at spiritual maturity. They believe they do not need any help. Perhaps at one time they _wanted_ to grow . . . but they would not pay the price necessary to take forward steps.

Paul reminds these "carnal" believers that their spiritual progress up to this point had come from following the standards set down in God's Word. He encourages them to go forward in the same way. They have been saved by grace, through faith, and not by their own works. So, they are to mature and progress according to those same standards.

God's goal is for us to become mature believers. He wants us to _grow up_ and get out of the "Peter Pan Syndrome." He wants us to be able to look back at our lives and see evidence of our continual growth. And He is never going to quit prompting us and motivating us to keep pressing on until He gets us where He wants us to be.

JOURNALING YOUR RESPONSE

What are some ways you can encourage others in their spiritual growth?

THE JOY OF HARMONY

Philippians 4:1–7

GETTING STARTED

What is one word of encouragement, advice, or guidance you would offer to a new Christian?

_____

_____

_____

_____

_____

_____

_____

_____

_____

_____

_____

_____

_____

_____

_____

_____

_____

_____

SETTING THE STAGE

Paul's exhortation in this next section of Philippians may reveal his primary reason for writing this letter to the church. As he states, "I implore Euodia and I implore Syntyche to be of the same mind in the Lord. And I urge you also, true companion, help these women who labored with me in the gospel, with Clement also, and the rest of my fellow workers" (4:2–3).

Paul's typical strategy for evangelizing in a new city was to go into the local synagogue and preach there. But Philippi didn't have a synagogue. So instead, Paul went to the river near the middle of the city where people gathered. There he met Lydia, a seller of purple cloth, who accepted Christ. She was the first of many women who joined with Paul and helped establish the church. Many of these women, like Lydia, were prosperous. They helped finance Paul's missionary journeys out of their love for the gospel and their love for him.

The Philippian church had grown since that time, and a few problems had developed. Chief among these issues was a conflict between Euodia and Syntyche, two women who had worked with Paul during his stay in Philippi. The name *Euodia* means "sweet fragrance," while *Syntyche* means "affable." So, Sweet Fragrance and Affable were not getting along in the church.

Paul had dealt with a similar problem in Ephesus. He urged the believers there to "walk worthy of the calling with which you were called, with all lowliness and gentleness, with longsuffering, bearing with one another in love" (Ephesians 4:1–2). Paul knew maintaining unity was hard work . . . but it was essential. We are all part of the body of Christ. So when there's a disruption or disunity in one part of the body, the entire body suffers.

In dealing with the division in the church of Philippi, Paul calls on his friends to help these women. He wants the problem resolved. His appeal is strong and his reasoning is clear. These women are members of the body of Christ, and they should not be divided.

EXPLORING THE TEXT

Be United, Joyful, and in Prayer (Philippians 4:1–4)

¹ Therefore, my beloved and longed-for brethren, my joy and crown, so stand fast in the Lord, beloved.

² I implore Euodia and I implore Syntyche to be of the same mind in the Lord. ³ And I urge you also, true companion, help these women who labored with me in the gospel, with Clement also, and the rest of my fellow workers, whose names are in the Book of Life.

⁴ Rejoice in the Lord always. Again I will say, rejoice!

1. In this final section of his letter, Paul continues his discussion on how the believers in Philippi can ensure their conduct is "worthy of the gospel of Christ" (1:27). What did he urge Euodia and Syntyche to do in this regard (see verses 2–3)?

2. What impact could such an attitude of rejoicing have on the conflict that threatened to divide the Philippian church (see verse 4)?

_____

_____

_____

_____

_____

_____

_____

_____

Praying with Thanksgiving (Philippians 4:5–7)

> ⁵ Let your gentleness be known to all men. The Lord is at hand.
> ⁶ Be anxious for nothing, but in everything by prayer and supplication, with thanksgiving, let your requests be made known to God;
> ⁷ and the peace of God, which surpasses all understanding, will guard your hearts and minds through Christ Jesus.

3. The phrase "be anxious" (Greek _merimnao_) can refer to worry, but it was often used in contexts where persecution was at stake. How is Paul thus instructing the believers to act in the face of the hostilities they were receiving in their culture (see verse 6)?

_____

_____

_____

_____

_____

4. The term "guard" (Greek *phroureo*) is also drawn from the arena of conflict and is used to refer to the actions of a military garrison stationed in a city. How does this describe the way in which God's peace will guard the believers when they face hostilities (see verse 7)?

_____

_____

_____

_____

_____

_____

_____

_____

_____

_____

GOING DEEPER

The apostle Paul was not unique in calling for the Philippians to rejoice even in the face of trials. Many other believers were facing persecution, and they were also feeling discouraged and disheartened. James wrote to one such community. In the epistle that bears his name, he reassures his readers that God sees their trials and has a purpose for allowing them to happen.

Profiting from Trials (James 1:2–8)

² My brethren, count it all joy when you fall into various trials, ³ knowing that the testing of your faith produces patience. ⁴ But let patience have its perfect work, that you may be perfect and complete, lacking nothing. ⁵ If any of you lacks wisdom, let him ask of God, who gives to all liberally and without reproach, and it will be given to him. ⁶ But let him ask in faith, with no doubting, for he who doubts is like

a wave of the sea driven and tossed by the wind. [7] For let not that man suppose that he will receive anything from the Lord; [8] he is a double-minded man, unstable in all his ways.

---

5. How does James say believers in Christ are to respond when they encounter trials (see verses 2–3)? How is this advice similar to the teaching that Paul offered in Philippians?

_____

_____

_____

_____

_____

_____

_____

_____

6. How does James say that trials develop our character? What should we do if we find that we are still "lacking" and need wisdom from God (see verses 4–6)?

_____

_____

_____

_____

_____

_____

_____

_____

The believers in Thessalonica were also experiencing persecution for their beliefs. In Paul's first letter to that church, he also offers an exhortation for them to rejoice and not be discouraged. In the following passage, Paul goes into more detail about exactly what is involved in rejoicing.

Do Not Render Evil for Evil (1 Thessalonians 5:14–22)

[14] Now we exhort you, brethren, warn those who are unruly, comfort the fainthearted, uphold the weak, be patient with all. [15] See that no one renders evil for evil to anyone, but always pursue what is good both for yourselves and for all.

[16] Rejoice always, [17] pray without ceasing, [18] in everything give thanks; for this is the will of God in Christ Jesus for you.

[19] Do not quench the Spirit. [20] Do not despise prophecies. [21] Test all things; hold fast what is good. [22] Abstain from every form of evil.

7. What does Paul say the believers should do when they are mistreated (see verses 14–15)?

8. What is the connection between rejoicing always, praying without ceasing, and giving thanks in everything (see verses 16–18)?

_____

_____

_____

_____

_____

_____

REVIEWING THE STORY

Paul begins the final section of his letter by reminding the believers that joy is found in harmony. He implores two members who are bickering to reconcile with one another and urges the church members to help them in this task. Paul then makes four exhortations. The believers are to (1) rejoice in the Lord always, (2) make their gentleness known to all, (3) not be anxious, and (4) make their requests known to God. As they do, they will receive the peace of God.

9. What words does Paul use to convey his affection for the Philippians (see Philippians 4:1)?

_____

_____

_____

_____

_____

_____

_____

10. What does Paul implore Euodia and Syntyche to do (see Philippians 4:2)?

_____

_____

_____

_____

_____

_____

_____

11. How should the believers let their requests be known to God (see Philippians 4:6)?

_____

_____

_____

_____

_____

_____

12. How does Paul describe the peace of God (see Philippians 4:7)?

_____

_____

_____

_____

_____

_____

APPLYING THE MESSAGE

13. What is the biggest obstacle to joy in your life?

_____

_____

_____

_____

_____

_____

_____

_____

_____

_____

_____

_____

14. What is a situation that you are facing in which you need the peace of God?

_____

_____

_____

_____

_____

_____

_____

_____

_____

_____

_____

REFLECTING ON THE MEANING

Euodia and Syntyche, the two women at the center of the Philippian controversy, were not getting along together. These women had been instrumental in aiding Paul in his early work in the church. So, he called on his friends in the church to "help these women" (4:3). He wanted the problem resolved. His appeal was strong, and his reasoning was clear. These women were members of the body of Christ . . . and they should not be divided.

Paul made three specific appeals as to why the women should reconcile. First, *they were united in their salvation*. Their names were written "in the Book of Life." In Revelation, we discover this is a book into which the names of every human being is entered. However, if the individual does not receive Christ as their Savior by the time they die, their name is blotted out of the book. Euodia and Syntyche had both chosen to follow Christ.

Second, *the women were united in spirit*. Paul says they should be "of the same mind" (verse 2) because the Holy Spirit lived within them. Paul is also talking about the spirit of humility and servanthood, which should have filled both of them. They had a unity in spirit.

Finally, *they were united in service*. Paul says, "These women . . . labored with me in the gospel" (verse 3). These women were not merely Christians. They were not just people who knew the Lord. They were women who *served* the Lord. They were unified in *salvation*, unified in *spirit*, and unified in *serving*. There was no reason therefore for them to be divided.

Jesus prayed that His followers would all be one (see John 17:21). We are all members of the body of Christ. When certain segments give in to disruption, disunity, arguments, and fights, it is not only displeasing to the Lord but also a poor reflection on His church. This is why we must work at unity. When something goes wrong or somebody gets upset, we have to work to make sure the situation is resolved so it does not do greater damage to the body of Christ.

Journaling Your Response

What is a situation in your life where you need to seek reconciliation and harmony?

THE JOY OF SECURITY

Philippians 4:8–13

GETTING STARTED

What is the biggest issue currently causing stress in your life?

_____

_____

_____

_____

_____

_____

_____

_____

_____

_____

_____

_____

_____

_____

_____

SETTING THE STAGE

The apostle Paul has just addressed the problem of anxiety the believers in Philippi were facing, which was likely happening as a result of persecution from their pagan neighbors. Paul also offered the prescription for their problem—which was prayer, supplication, and thanksgiving. If the believers followed this counsel, they would receive a peace from God that surpassed all understanding . . . and their hearts and minds would be guarded in Christ.

Few of us today are experiencing anxiety as a result of being persecuted for our faith. However, many of us experience anxiety as a result of the many trials and struggles that confront us each day. While these worries vary from person to person, studies show the top five concerns that cause stress are (1) financial debts, (2) health, (3) low energy levels, (4) savings and retirement fears, and (5) getting older. Other studies show that high levels of stress can, in turn, lead to many physical, mental, and spiritual health issues in people.

The good news is that the program Paul outlines in this next section of his letter is just as effective in treating our anxieties today as it was for the believers in Philippi in the first century. This program involves adopting the *right thinking* that will lead to taking the *right actions*. In the Greek, the term that Paul used for *anxious* actually comes from two other Greek words, one that means *mind* and one that means *divided*. Anxiety is thus a state of having a divided mind—going back and forth between what is and isn't true. So, the remedy is to reprogram our mind so we stay focused only on what is true.

It is not enough for us to just remove our negative thoughts through prayer. We also have to replace those thoughts with something positive. As we do this, we come to discover the joy that can be found in security, knowing that God is in charge and we are safe in Him.

EXPLORING THE TEXT

Meditate on These Things (Philippians 4:8–9)

---

⁸ Finally, brethren, whatever things are true, whatever things are
noble, whatever things are just, whatever things are pure, whatever

things are lovely, whatever things are of good report, if there is any virtue and if there is anything praiseworthy—meditate on these things. [9] The things which you learned and received and heard and saw in me, these do, and the God of peace will be with you.

---

1. Paul has just instructed the Philippians to turn to God in prayer when they were feeling anxious and to look to Him to provide His perfect peace. What additional step does Paul say believers need to take as it relates to their thoughts (see verse 8)?

_____

_____

_____

_____

_____

2. There is a big difference between meditating on virtues and living them out. What did Paul remind the believers that he had done when he was with them (see verse 9)?

_____

_____

_____

_____

The Generosity of the Church (Philippians 4:10–13)

[10] But I rejoiced in the Lord greatly that now at last your care for me has flourished again; though you surely did care, but you lacked opportunity. [11] Not that I speak in regard to need, for I have learned in whatever state I am, to be content: [12] I know how to be abased, and I know how to abound. Everywhere and in all things I have learned

both to be full and to be hungry, both to abound and to suffer need.
¹³ I can do all things through Christ who strengthens me.

_____

3. Paul begins to close his letter by thanking the Philippians for the monetary gift they sent through Epaphroditus. Paul was grateful for the gift, but what brought him true joy (see verse 10)?

_____

_____

_____

_____

_____

4. What does Paul say that he had learned when it comes to his needs? What truth was he trying to convey to the Philippians through his example (see verses 11–13)?

_____

_____

_____

_____

_____

_____

GOING DEEPER

Paul's acknowledgment of the Philippians' gift can seem a bit begrudging to modern readers—a "thank you, but I didn't really need it," type of response. However, Paul was simply following the protocol of his day for expressing appreciation, and he also uses the opportunity to stress it is *God* who ultimately provides our security in this life. In the Old Testament, we find the prophet Jeremiah reminding the people of Israel of this same truth.

Trust in the Lord (Jeremiah 17:7–10)

⁷ "Blessed is the man who trusts in the LORD,

And whose hope is the LORD.

⁸ For he shall be like a tree planted by the waters,

Which spreads out its roots by the river,

And will not fear when heat comes;

But its leaf will be green,

And will not be anxious in the year of drought,

Nor will cease from yielding fruit.

⁹ "The heart is deceitful above all things,

And desperately wicked;

Who can know it?

¹⁰ I, the LORD, search the heart,

I test the mind,

Even to give every man according to his ways,

According to the fruit of his doings.

5. What does the Lord say happens to those who place their trust in Him? How does God promise to provide security and strength to those who rely on Him (see verses 7–8)?

_____

_____

_____

_____

6. Why is it foolish to place our trust in human wisdom? How does the Lord reveal our true intentions (see verses 9–10)?

_____

_____

_____

_____

Paul's admonition for the believers in Philippi to reprogram their minds to focus on the things of God rather than the worries of this world is also found in Jesus' teachings. In the following passage, Jesus draws His listeners' attention to the natural world in order to make a profound point about worry. In the process, He delivers one of the most comforting lessons on God's provision, security, and care for us in all of Scripture.

Do Not Worry (Matthew 6:25–34)

[25] "Therefore I say to you, do not worry about your life, what you will eat or what you will drink; nor about your body, what you will put on. Is not life more than food and the body more than clothing? [26] Look at the birds of the air, for they neither sow nor reap nor gather into barns; yet your heavenly Father feeds them. Are you not of more value than they? [27] Which of you by worrying can add one cubit to his stature?

[28] "So why do you worry about clothing? Consider the lilies of the field, how they grow: they neither toil nor spin; [29] and yet I say to you that even Solomon in all his glory was not arrayed like one of these. [30] Now if God so clothes the grass of the field, which today is, and tomorrow is thrown into the oven, will He not much more clothe you, O you of little faith?

[31] "Therefore do not worry, saying, 'What shall we eat?' or 'What shall we drink?' or 'What shall we wear?' [32] For after all these things the Gentiles seek. For your heavenly Father knows that you need all these things. [33] But seek first the kingdom of God and His righteousness, and all these things shall be added to you. [34] Therefore do not worry about tomorrow, for tomorrow will worry about its own things. Sufficient for the day is its own trouble."

7. According to Jesus, what concerns and fears should *not* occupy the minds of His followers? What does Jesus' example of the "birds of the air" reveal about God's care for them—and, by extension, to each one of us (see verses 25–27)?

_____

_____

_____

_____

8. The Jewish people had the advantage of God's revelation, and He expected them to have a different outlook on their circumstances than that of the Gentiles. What should have been their attitude toward their future security (see verses 31–34)?

_____

_____

_____

_____

Reviewing the Story

Paul advises the Philippian believers to deal with worry by reprogramming their minds to dwell on things that are true, noble, just, pure, lovely, good, and praiseworthy whenever they feel things are spiraling out of their control. He encourages them to remember his teachings and example when they are faced with situations that make them fearful. He closes by thanking them for their gift, but notes that he has learned to be content in all situations—both in want and in plenty—and encourages them to likewise look to Christ for their strength and security.

9. On what does Paul instruct the believers in Philippi to meditate (see Philippians 4:8)?

_____

_____

_____

_____

10. What does Paul say will be the result if the believers follow the example that he set when he was with them (see Philippians 4:9)?

11. What does Paul say causes him to rejoice greatly in the Lord (see Philippians 4:10)?

12. What ultimate "life lesson" had Paul learned (see Philippians 4:11)?

APPLYING THE MESSAGE

13. What are some things you have been tempted to put your trust in other than God?

14. What are some areas that you need to commit to God today?

_____

_____

_____

_____

_____

REFLECTING ON THE MEANING

Genuine guarantees are rare in life. For instance, if you were to go to the doctor and say, "I've got this problem," he wouldn't say, "Take this, and I promise you will get better." Rather, the doctor would tell you to try a treatment and then report back on how you are feeling.

However, as we see in this section of Philippians, the apostle Paul was not shy about offering a _guarantee_ to his readers if they followed the course of action that he was prescribing. He states that if they make their anxieties known to God, ask for His help, and reprogram their thoughts, "the God of peace" will be with them (4:9). Paul is saying, in essence, "If you do what the Word of God tells you to do, you will be victorious over worry."

Paul also guarantees that not only will God give us His peace, but he will also provide strength to "do all things" (verse 13). If you have ever been rocked by circumstances and witnessed God intervene to give you peace and strength, you know how hard this idea is to explain to someone else—especially someone who is not a Christian. Likely, the person will look at you as if he or she has no idea what you are talking about. How could anyone have peace in the midst of suffering, loss, or uncertainty?

We cannot explain God's intervention, because it involves a peace that "surpasses all understanding" (verse 7). It can only be experienced to be known. But still, it is guaranteed to happen. The God of peace will make His presence known through His comfort and encouragement. He will draw near to us when problems come in ways that we cannot understand. We will sense His presence like never before—and stand secure.

JOURNALING YOUR RESPONSE

When have you experienced the peace of God in your life?

THE JOY OF SERENITY

Philippians 4:14–23

GETTING STARTED

At what point in your life were you most content?

SETTING THE STAGE

The final section of Paul's letter to the Philippians includes a statement of gratitude for their continued support. As we have seen, the believers had sent Epaphroditus to deliver funds to Paul to aid his ministry. The apostle was thankful, but he was careful to say that he had learned to rely on God during his time of need and look to Him for contentment.

The word content in this context means "self-sufficient." Greek philosophers of the day known as the Stoics had a great way of looking at this. They believed people should be sufficient in and unto themselves in all things. When they were asked who is wealthy, they would say, "The one who is content with the least, for self-sufficiency is nature's wealth."

But for Paul, this sufficiency did not come from ourselves. As he wrote to the Corinthians, "Not that we are sufficient of ourselves to think of anything as being from ourselves, but our sufficiency is from God" (2 Corinthians 3:5). The things of this world that we are told are necessary for contentment ultimately don't matter. But the things that get overlooked in the pursuit of contentment—such as our faith in God—are of vital importance.

So, as Paul comes to the end of his letter, he provides a tutorial on how we can develop a true spirit of contentment. After all, this is not something with which we are born. Contentment is not in our genes . . . it is something we must learn and master. The apostle Paul had figured out the secret, and in this closing section he shares that knowledge with us.

EXPLORING THE TEXT

An Example in Giving (Philippians 4:14–17)

> [14] Nevertheless you have done well that you shared in my distress.
> [15] Now you Philippians know also that in the beginning of the gospel, when I departed from Macedonia, no church shared with me concerning giving and receiving but you only. [16] For even in Thessalonica

you sent aid once and again for my necessities. ¹⁷ Not that I seek the gift, but I seek the fruit that abounds to your account.

---

1. In the culture of Paul's day, gifts were intended to bring honor to the giver. What did it say about the Philippians that they chose to give gifts to someone who had been disgraced and imprisoned (see verses 14–16)?

_____

_____

_____

_____

_____

_____

_____

_____

2. The Philippian believers' relationship with Paul reflected their relationship with God. What was more meaningful to Paul than the gift itself (see verse 17)?

_____

_____

_____

_____

_____

_____

_____

_____

_____

God, Our Provider (Philippians 4:18–23)

¹⁸ Indeed I have all and abound. I am full, having received from Epaphroditus the things sent from you, a sweet-smelling aroma, an acceptable sacrifice, well pleasing to God. ¹⁹ And my God shall supply all your need according to His riches in glory by Christ Jesus. ²⁰ Now to our God and Father be glory forever and ever. Amen.

²¹ Greet every saint in Christ Jesus. The brethren who are with me greet you. ²² All the saints greet you, but especially those who are of Caesar's household.

²³ The grace of our Lord Jesus Christ be with you all. Amen.

---

3. According to the customs of the day, those who received gifts were indebted to the givers. Yet Paul knows that from his prison cell, he will be incapable of repaying their generosity. How does he address this issue (see verses 18–20)?

4. Paul closes by sending greetings from "those who are of Caesar's household" (verse 22). These are likely members of the imperial administration in the city where Paul was imprisoned. What does this say about the reach of the gospel?

_____

_____

_____

_____

_____

_____

_____

GOING DEEPER

The apostle Paul had no reason to feel any contentment by human standards. He had been misunderstood, maligned, and mistreated throughout his ministry. Paul could have become bitter at any point, but instead of fretting over evildoers or his misfortunes, he chose to seek contentment in Christ. In the following psalm, King David likewise urges us to find our peace and joy in God, knowing that He will deal with the workers of iniquity in our lives.

The Heritage of the Righteous (Psalm 37:1–6)

> [1] Do not fret because of evildoers,
> Nor be envious of the workers of iniquity.
> [2] For they shall soon be cut down like the grass,
> And wither as the green herb.
>
> [3] Trust in the LORD, and do good;
> Dwell in the land, and feed on His faithfulness.

⁴ Delight yourself also in the Lord,

And He shall give you the desires of your heart.

⁵ Commit your way to the Lord,

Trust also in Him,

And He shall bring it to pass.

⁶ He shall bring forth your righteousness as the light,

And your justice as the noonday.

---

5. Seeing good things happen to bad people often confuses and discourages good people. What is our best strategy when confusion or discouragement sets in (see verses 1–3)?

_____

_____

_____

_____

_____

_____

6. What happens when our desires spring from our relationship with God (see verses 4–5)?

_____

_____

_____

_____

_____

_____

Wait Patiently for the Lord (Psalm 37:7–11)

⁷ Rest in the LORD, and wait patiently for Him;
Do not fret because of him who prospers in his way,
Because of the man who brings wicked schemes to pass.
⁸ Cease from anger, and forsake wrath;
Do not fret—it only causes harm.
⁹ For evildoers shall be cut off;

But those who wait on the LORD,
They shall inherit the earth.
¹⁰ For yet a little while and the wicked shall be no more;
Indeed, you will look carefully for his place,
But it shall be no more.
¹¹ But the meek shall inherit the earth,
And shall delight themselves in the abundance of peace.

---

7. How do we prevent wicked schemers and evildoers from being able to push our emotional buttons (see verses 7–9)?

8. What promise do we receive about the ultimate fate of the wicked? What is the promise made to the "meek" or those model an attitude of humility (see verses 10–11)?

_____

_____

_____

_____

_____

_____

_____

REVIEWING THE STORY

The apostle Paul closes his letter by commending the Philippians for their generosity in caring for his needs. He expresses that he is content in spite of his situation, calls their gift "an acceptable sacrifice" that is "well pleasing to God" (4:18), and assures them that God will provide for all their needs. He ends with personal greetings from himself, his coworkers, and even members of "Caesar's household" who had become believers in Christ.

9. What had the Philippian believers done well (see Philippians 4:14)?

_____

_____

_____

_____

_____

_____

_____

_____

10. What does Paul seek from God for the Philippians (see Philippians 4:17)?

_____

_____

_____

_____

_____

_____

_____

11. How did God receive the Philippians' generosity toward Paul (see Philippians 4:18)?

_____

_____

_____

_____

_____

_____

_____

12. What does Paul say to indicate that God was blessing his efforts to share the gospel in Rome (see Philippians 4:22)?

_____

_____

_____

_____

_____

_____

_____

APPLYING THE MESSAGE

13. What changes can you make to your priorities and approach to life in order to be more content in the Lord?

_____

_____

_____

_____

_____

_____

_____

_____

_____

14. How can you express your God-given contentment in ways that inspire others?

_____

_____

_____

_____

_____

_____

_____

_____

_____

_____

REFLECTING ON THE MEANING

Paul's words in this closing passage remind us of three things about contentment. First, *contentment begins with a thorough inventory*. We need to have a complete understanding of God's blessings in our lives. That involves identifying the talents, gifts, and abilities He has given us. It involves identifying our allies, mentors, teachers, friends, and family members—the people who love us, encourage us, and expect big things from us. In other words, it involves identifying the people God has placed in our lives to make us better people.

A thorough inventory also involves identifying basic needs that are met for us every day—such as food, shelter, clothing, transportation, and safety. It involves identifying the "luxuries" that we often take for granted. And, saving the best for last, it involves identifying the spiritual blessings that we enjoy as followers of Christ—the assurance of our salvation, our personal relationship with the Lord, the guidance of the Holy Spirit, the wisdom and encouragement of Scripture, and 24–7 access to God through prayer, to name just a few. The more clearly we understand just how much we have, the easier it will be to find contentment in what God has done for us.

Second, *contentment requires a shift in focus*. It is tempting to train our attention on those individuals who seem to have more than we possess. But that is a problem, because the seeds of envy require little nourishing to produce the fruit of discontentment. Instead of asking why we don't seem to have as much as a certain privileged few, a better approach is to ask why we seem to have so much more than so many others. Knowing that we are unworthy of the blessings we enjoy primes our hearts so that contentment and joy can take root.

Finally, *contentment changes lives—and not just our own*. To be content is to reach the point where we stop trying to get our own needs met and start trying to meet the needs of others. God doesn't bless us so that we can indulge in what we have. Rather, He blesses us so that we can use what we have to bless others.

Journaling Your Response

What do you think a thorough inventory would reveal about God's blessings in your life?

LEADER'S GUIDE

Thank you for choosing to lead your group through this study from Dr. David Jeremiah on *The Letter to the Philippians*. Being a group leader has its own rewards, and it is our prayer that your walk with the Lord will deepen through this experience. During the twelve lessons in this study, you and your group will read selected passages from Philippians, explore key themes in the letter based on teachings from Dr. Jeremiah, and review questions that will encourage group discussion. There are multiple components in this section that can help you structure your lessons and discussion time, so please be sure to read and consider each one.

BEFORE YOU BEGIN

Before your first meeting, make sure you and your group are well-versed with the content of the lesson. Group members should have their own copy of *The Letter to the Philippians* study guide prior to the first meeting so they can follow along and record their answers, thoughts, and insights. After the first week, you may wish to assign the study guide lesson as homework prior to the group meeting and then use the meeting time to discuss the content in the lesson.

To ensure everyone has a chance to participate in the discussion, the ideal size for a group is around eight to ten people. If there are more than ten people, break up the bigger group into smaller subgroups. Make sure the members are committed to participating each week, as this will help create stability and help you better prepare the structure of the meeting.

At the beginning of each week's study, start with the opening Getting Started question to introduce the topic you will be discussing. The members should answer briefly, as the goal is just for them to have an idea of the subject in their minds as you go over the lesson. This will allow the members to become engaged and ready to interact with the rest of the group.

After reviewing the lesson, try to initiate a free-flowing discussion. Invite group members to bring questions and insights they may have discovered to the next meeting, especially if they were unsure of the meaning of some parts of the lesson. Be prepared to discuss how biblical truth applies to the world we live in today.

WEEKLY PREPARATION

As the group leader, here are a few things that you can do to prepare for each meeting:

- *Be thoroughly familiar with the material in the lesson.* Make sure that you understand the content of each lesson so you know how to structure the group time and are prepared to lead the group discussion.

- *Decide, ahead of time, which questions you want to discuss.* Depending on how much time you have each week, you may not be able to reflect on every question. Select specific questions that you feel will evoke the best discussion.

- *Take prayer requests.* At the end of your discussion, take prayer requests from your group members and then pray for one another.

STRUCTURING THE DISCUSSION TIME

There are several ways to structure the duration of the study. You can choose to cover each lesson individually, for a total of twelve weeks of group meetings, or you can combine two lessons together per week, for a total of six weeks of group meetings. The following charts illustrate these options:

TWELVE-WEEK FORMAT

Week	Lessons Covered	Reading
1	The Joy of Community	*Philippians 1:1–11*
2	The Joy of Adversity	*Philippians 1:12–18*
3	The Joy of Integrity	*Philippians 1:19–30*
4	The Joy of Unity	*Philippians 2:1–11*
5	The Joy of Responsibility	*Philippians 2:12–18*
6	The Joy of Ministry	*Philippians 2:19–30*
7	The Joy of Humility	*Philippians 3:1–11*
8	The Joy of Victory	*Philippians 3:12–16*
9	The Joy of Maturity	*Philippians 3:17–21*
10	The Joy of Harmony	*Philippians 4:1–7*
11	The Joy of Security	*Philippians 4:8–13*
12	The Joy of Serenity	*Philippians 4:14–23*

SIX-WEEK FORMAT

Week	Lessons Covered	Reading
1	The Joy of Community / The Joy of Adversity	*Philippians 1:1–18*
2	The Joy of Integrity / The Joy of Unity	*Philippians 1:19–2:11*
3	The Joy of Responsibility / The Joy of Ministry	*Philippians 2:12–30*
4	The Joy of Humility / The Joy of Victory	*Philippians 3:1–16*
5	The Joy of Maturity / The Joy of Harmony	*Philippians 3:17–4:7*
6	The Joy of Security / The Joy of Serenity	*Philippians 4:8–23*

In regard to organizing your time when planning your group Bible study, the following two schedules, for sixty minutes and ninety minutes, can give you a structure for the lesson:

Section	60 Minutes	90 Minutes
Welcome: Members arrive and get settled	5 minutes	10 minutes
Getting Started Question: Prepares the group for interacting with one another	10 minutes	10 minutes
Message: Review the lesson	15 minutes	25 minutes
Discussion: Discuss questions in the lesson	25 minutes	35 minutes
Review and Prayer: Review the key points of the lesson and have a closing time of prayer	5 minutes	10 minutes

As the group leader, it is up to you to keep track of the time and keep things moving according to your schedule. If your group is having a good discussion, don't feel the need to stop and move on to the next question. Remember, the purpose is to pull together ideas and share unique insights on the lesson. Encourage everyone to participate, but don't be concerned if certain group members are more quiet. They may just be internally reflecting on the questions and need time to process their ideas before they can share them.

GROUP DYNAMICS

Leading a group study can be a rewarding experience for you and your group members—but that doesn't mean there won't be challenges. Certain members may feel uncomfortable discussing topics that they consider very personal and might be afraid of being called on. Some members might have disagreements on specific issues. To help prevent these scenarios, consider the following ground rules:

- If someone has a question that may seem off topic, suggest that it be discussed at another time, or ask the group if they are okay with addressing that topic.

- If someone asks a question you don't know the answer to, confess that you don't know and move on. If you feel comfortable, invite other group members to give their opinions or share their comments based on personal experience.
- If you feel like a couple of people are talking much more than others, direct questions to people who may not have shared yet. You could even ask the more dominating members to help draw out the quiet ones.
- When there is a disagreement, encourage the group members to process the matter in love. Invite members from opposing sides to evaluate their opinions and consider the ideas of the other members. Lead the group through Scripture that addresses the topic, and look for common ground.

When issues arise, encourage your group to think of Scripture: "Love one another" (John 13:34), "If it is possible, as much as it depends on you, live peaceably with all men" (Romans 12:18), and, "Be swift to hear, slow to speak, slow to wrath" (James 1:19).

ABOUT
Dr. David Jeremiah and Turning Point

Dr. David Jeremiah is the founder of Turning Point, a ministry committed to providing Christians with sound Bible teaching relevant to today's changing times through radio and television broadcasts, audio series, books, and live events. Dr. Jeremiah's teaching on topics such as family, prayer, worship, angels, and biblical prophecy forms the foundation of Turning Point.

David and his wife, Donna, reside in El Cajon, California, where he serves as the senior pastor of Shadow Mountain Community Church. David and Donna have four children and twelve grandchildren.

In 1982, Dr. Jeremiah brought the same solid teaching to San Diego television that he shares weekly with his congregation. Shortly thereafter, Turning Point expanded its ministry to radio. Dr. Jeremiah's inspiring messages can now be heard worldwide on radio, television, and the internet.

Because Dr. Jeremiah desires to know his listening audience, he travels nationwide holding ministry rallies and spiritual enrichment conferences that touch the hearts and lives of many people. According to Dr. Jeremiah, "At some point in time, everyone reaches a turning point; and for every person, that moment is unique, an experience to hold onto forever. There's so much changing in today's world that sometimes it's difficult to choose the right path. Turning Point offers people an understanding of God's Word and seeks to make a difference in their lives."

Dr. Jeremiah has authored numerous books, including *Escape the Coming Night* (Revelation), *The Handwriting on the Wall* (Daniel), *Overcoming Loneliness*, *Prayer—The Great Adventure*, *God in You* (Holy

Spirit), *When Your World Falls Apart, Slaying the Giants in Your Life, My Heart's Desire, Hope for Today, Captured by Grace, Signs of Life, What in the World Is Going On?, The Coming Economic Armageddon, I Never Thought I'd See the Day!, God Loves You: He Always Has—He Always Will, Agents of the Apocalypse, Agents of Babylon, Revealing the Mysteries of Heaven, People Are Asking . . . Is This the End?, A Life Beyond Amazing, Overcomer, The Book of Signs,* and *Everything You Need.*

New Bible Study Series from Dr. David Jeremiah

The Jeremiah Bible Study Series captures Dr. David Jeremiah's forty-plus years of commitment to teaching the whole Word of God. Each volume contains twelve lessons for individuals and groups to explore what the Bible says, what it meant to the people at the time it was written, and what it means to us today. Out of his lifelong ministry of *delivering the unchanging Word of God to an ever-changing world*, Dr. Jeremiah has written this Bible-strong study series focused not on causes, current events, or politics, but on the solid truth of Scripture.

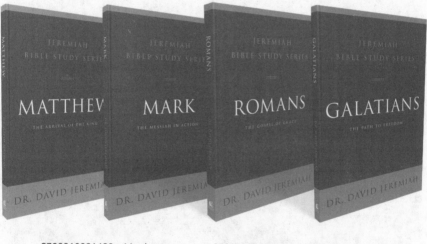

THOMAS NELSON
Since 1798

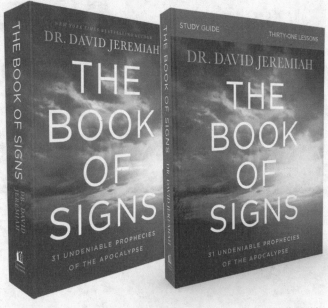